TIBET: ENDURING SPIR
EXPLOITED LAND

TIBET: ENDURING SPIRIT EXPLOITED LAND

Robert Z. Apte and Andrés R. Edwards

Foreword and Poem by

The Dalai Lama

HEARTSFIRE BOOKS

Library of Congress Cataloging-in-Publication Data

Apte, Robert Z., 1924–

Tibet: enduring spirit, exploited land / by Robert Z. Apte and Andrés R. Edwards; foreword by His Holiness the Dalai Lama

p. cm.

Includes bibliographical references and index.

ISBN 1-889797-11-1 (cloth) : $29.95

1. Tibet (China) I. Edwards, Andrés R., 1959– II. Title.

DS786.A73 1998 97–121948

951'.5--DC21 CIP

Cover photo by Galen Rowell
Cover design by Cisneros Design
Book design and text composition by John Cole GRAPHIC DESIGNER
Printed in Canada by Transcontinental Printing & Graphics
Text is set in Adobe Goudy

First edition 1998
10 9 8 7 6 5 4 3 2 1

Heartsfire Books: 800.988.5170
500 N. Guadalupe Street, Suite G465
Santa Fe, New Mexico 87501 USA

If you are unable to order this book from your local bookseller, you may order directly from the publisher. Quantity discounts for organizations are available.

We dedicate *Tibet: Enduring Spirit, Exploited Land*

to all the nomads, semi-nomads, and farmers of Tibet

who have forged the foundation of the Tibetan culture.

Through their wisdom, fortitude, and tenacity they have

endured and thrived on the roof of the world.

Contents

Acknowledgments

This book was produced by almost completely voluntary effort. The authors wish to thank and to acknowledge the numerous organizations and people who played a role in its development.

But first we must acknowledge the enthusiasm that energized and propelled us to write the book. We and the others who have contributed to it have been unwavering in our determination to lend support to the Tibetan people—those who have suffered from a brutal occupation. In the early stages of gathering material for the book, His Holiness The Dalai Lama was consulted about aspects of the work. There was a convergence of His vision and that of the authors' as to its nature and significance. This energy to persevere in spite of delays draws, in part, from the support and encouragement received from His Holiness.

We must recognize our wives, Evelyn L. Apte, and Rochelle Edwards for their support and help in furthering the project. Evelyn Apte became involved from the onset, and fully participated in the book planning and in carrying out the initial interviews with the nomads in Dharamsala. Her sensitivity to, and observations of, the Tibetans during the interview process, and her literary advice as the book proceeded are much appreciated. Rochelle Edwards's review of the manuscript during the writing was especially helpful as was her support for the work as a whole.

The relationship that developed with the staff of The Department of Information and International Relations in Dharamsala, India, provided us with direct access to important information on the growing negative impact on the environment in Tibet. Tempa Tsering, the Department Director, was especially helpful in making available the rich resources of his staff by providing interviewing space, consultation, and translators. During a period when limited personnel were available, we still received the help we needed.

Tenzin Atisha, Head of the Environment and Development Desk, greatly extended his services to accommodate our needs for information and access to former nomads and farmers. We found him seriously devoted to furthering education about the ecological problem in Tibet. He played a major role in setting up the interviewing project with Tibetan nomads and farmers, and in translating the interviews from Tibetan into English.

Tsering Tsomo played a leading role as the project director of the field survey. She set up the interviews, trained and supervised the interviewers and translations of the tape recordings, and generally oversaw the field survey project through each phase. We heartily acknowledge her important role in the project and thank her for her efforts.

Appreciation goes to Tashi Gyaltsen, abbot of the Dip Tse-Chock-Ling Monastery in Dharamsala, for his willingness to be interviewed—the first time by a non-Tibetan—and for providing useful insights into the origins of the Tibetans' special relationship to the environment. The opportunity provided us to interview Dr. Tenzin Choedrak about his observations before and after the occupation is especially appreciated.

We also wish to acknowledge and thank the Tibetans who were selected by Tsering Tsomo to carry out and translate the interviews. A significant part of the text was shaped by their interviewing skills. We acknowledge here, as well, the participation of the six nomads and farmers we interviewed (and whose names have been changed in this book to protect family members remaining in Tibet). We acknowledge the many other Tibetans in exile who generously participated in interviews, with little personal gain.

All of the above, we met and worked with in Dharamsala. Also helpful to us in Dharamsala were Rinchen Kando, His Holiness, and the Rinpoche with whom we discussed the planning and writing of our book.

While in Kathmandu, we collected information at the Tibetan Refugee Reception Center. We wish to thank their staff for the help received in meeting with and interviewing Tibetan families who had just come over the border from Tibet. Many were still in a state of physical shock from the hardship they had just endured, but still willingly participated in the interviews.

Our acknowledgment and appreciation goes to the photographers (See photographers' credits, p. 172) in various parts of the world who voluntarily provided us with photographs to use in the book. Although not all those photographers' works are represented in the book, we appreciate their interest and their willingness to share their work without compensation.

A significant amount of assistance and support came from individuals living in the United States, mostly residents of the San Francisco Bay Area, and members of the Bay Area Friends of Tibet (BAFoT). It was Ed Lazar, on the Board of BAFoT, who alerted us to the deterioration of the Tibetan environment and spurred on the effort leading to this book. The Committee for Education on Tibet participated in shaping the form and direction of this book. Their support and generous help of the members is acknowledged here: Barbara Banks, Ed Sobel, Jan Potts, Greg Alling, Janet Quartieri, Tashi Norbu, Garry Griffiths, Justin Lowe, Mark Vaz, D'Arcy Richardson, Peter Overmire, Glen Gilbert, Darcy Ellman. It was Janet Quartieri who provided us a wonderful service in helping to organize the information received from the field study.

Special acknowledgment goes to Carol Fields, who willingly served as a "reality check" in regard to both the process and content of the text. Her comprehensive but unpublished literature search and literature review on flora and fauna in Tibet provided a valuable document on the state of Tibet's environment before its occupation. This work was very useful in the process of writing this book.

Appreciation is also given to Lama Kunga Rimpoche of the Ewam Choden Buddhist Center in Kensington, California, for his insights into the nature of environmental education among Tibetans.

Our appreciation also goes to John Ackerly of the International Campaign for Tibet in Washington D.C., for his comments and encouragement. Erin Potts, who had done an internship in his office and heads the Milarepa Fund, generously provided us with needed information.

We would like to thank the person who donated the map of Tibet.

When it came to the writing of the text, two names come to mind as individuals who were especially helpful. With his mindfulness of ecology, Craig Comstock contributed to expanding our notions of the future of Tibet and to realizing the potential significance of the concept of the Dalai Lama's Zone of Peace. Jeff Greenwald, with the pen of a poet, helped us early on to find some balance between presenting Tibet as the idyllic land—the harsh foreboding awesome land—and as a land where the power, mystery, magic, and beauty, are found in the values of the people.

Finally, we would like to extend our appreciation to Sara Held, Claude Saks, and John Cole who recognized the importance of this topic and nourished it to its completion.

Preface

From the beginning of recorded history, we Tibetans have lived in harmony with nature. The land was regarded as holy. The Buddhist scriptures taught us not to harm plant and animal life, and to recognize the interdependence of all sentient beings.

In their daily lives, nomads and farmers practiced a remarkable land ethic. Until recently, no one bothered to write about the successes and failures of nomadic and farming practices in Tibet. Their lifestyle changed little over time, and their livelihood, as far as we can determine, had minimal impact on the environment. Explorers in the nineteenth and twentieth centuries recorded Tibet's bountiful wildlife.

Now, almost a half century after the Chinese invasion of Tibet, we have seen the land that we so ardently protected, severely exploited. Our forests and animals have fallen victim to Chinese axes and guns. The rivers and lakes we have revered have given way to the Chinese need to feed their own people and to their drive toward industrial development. The nomads' and farmers' time-proven methods of land and range management have come under attack over the years. Many Tibetans have fled their native land in order to survive.

With the assistance from dedicated people worldwide and the advance of telecommunications, the situation in Tibet is gaining recognition on the world stage. The authors of *Tibet: Enduring Spirit, Exploited Land* have vividly captured the proven practices of Tibetan nomads and farmers on one of the most remote regions on Earth. In addition, through the voices of Tibetans and stunning photographs, the book describes the extraordinary way Tibetans have successfully managed to live on the "roof of the world." We hope this way of life survives and serves as an example to other environmentally threatened regions of the world.

TENZIN ATISHA
Tibet Government-In-Exile
Environment & Development Desk,
Department of Information & International Relations

The Dalai Lama

The people of Tibet for centuries have adhered to spiritual and environmental values in order to maintain the delicate balance of life. Tibetans have a great respect for all forms of life. The concepts of non-violence, compassion, and the interdependence of living and non-living elements of the earth, teach us to be more caring and more concerned about others and our surroundings. This belief is further strengthened by the Tibetan Buddhists' traditional adherence to the principle of self-contentment: that the environment should be used to fulfill one's needs, and not greed.

Prior to China's invasion in 1949, Tibet was a beautiful and unspoiled wilderness sanctuary in a unique natural environment. Unfortunately, during the last few decades, Tibet's wildlife and environment has been severely damaged and in many places the damage have been irreparable. The unique Tibetan way of life has been trampled upon by a materialistic and atheist attitude. The environment of Tibet is now plagued with rampant deforestation and excessive mining. It is further threatened by the increasing number of Chinese settlers pouring into Tibet for short-term economic gains.

The significance of the Tibetan Plateau could be understood from the fact that it is the source of ten major rivers, which are the lifeline of millions of people living in Asia. What happens in Tibet has a direct bearing on the lives of millions of people living downstream. The environmental balance of Tibet also affects the global weather pattern as recent scientific research shows.

At this crucial stage, Tibetans in Tibet and in exile need, more than ever before, the assistance of the global community in their endeavour to protect their homeland.

Tibet's environment, with its distinct cultural heritage and national identity, can only be preserved if a mutually agreeable political solution is found to the Tibetan problem. I have been making every effort over the years to facilitate negotiations with the Chinese government. I appeal to various governments, organizations, and individuals to bring China to the negotiating table. I welcome this book and am sure that it will help in creating more awareness among the people about the tragic ecological plight of Tibet and move them to help save Tibet.

TENZIN GYATSO
The Dalai Lama

Why Care about Tibet?

For much of this past century, Tibet has been glamorized as a Shangri-La—a place of impenetrable mystery, isolated on an exotic plateau on the roof of the world, where few Westerners ever managed to explore. More recently, however, this romantic image has given way to the reality of a landmass consisting of approximately one million square miles and a culture that has been oppressed and virtually obliterated by its powerful neighbor to the east. In the West, we are becoming increasingly aware of human rights abuses in Tibet by the Chinese government but we are less aware of the ongoing environmental destruction that has been occurring since the Chinese invasion almost fifty years ago.

China's hunger for development is wreaking havoc on the environment of the Tibetan Plateau and, in the process, destroying a culture which has, until recently, flourished under harsh conditions for thousands of years. However, the world community cannot expect to resolve the Tibetan situation by looking at Tibet in isolation, or even at only Tibet and China. In many respects, the situation we describe in *Tibet: Enduring Spirit, Exploited Land* serves as a microcosm of what is transpiring across the world. Tibet, like many other developing regions, is experiencing the effects of uncontrolled growth spurred by industrialized nations.

In order to understand Tibet's situation we need to view the issues in a regional, and even global, context and to look at how various issues are connected. The Tibetan human rights issue, for example, is connected to the political structure in China, which, in turn, is connected to population pressures, education, foreign trade, the viability of the environment, and numerous other factors. Because all these problems are interconnected, and since the relationships among them are constantly changing, the whole complex of problems needs to be considered simultaneously.

Tibetans, like other indigenous peoples, have always understood that their interdependence with the environment is essential to their survival and well-being. Seeing themselves as caretakers of the land, Tibetans have recognized their responsibility to maintain the balance of their ecology. The Tibetans' wisdom is based on a subsistence approach to using the land, coupled with a respect for the limitations imposed by their environment. In the simplest terms, this means not wasting or abusing what nature provides—from wildlife to vegetation, soil, water, and air. Their sensitive understanding of the links in the web of life gives nomads and farmers an appreciation for the recurring patterns in nature and the limitations of all living systems.

One of the keys to Tibetan coexistence with the environment is to embrace a long-term view in making decisions that consider effects on succeeding generations, as well as reflecting the Buddhist acceptance of the cyclical nature of all living things. This approach, coupled with a keen knowledge of the natural world, has marked Tibetan experience through thousands of years. Nomads and farmers learned to listen to the land and perform activities that sustain, rather than deplete, the viability of ecosystems in the Tibetan Plateau.

As we prepare for the dawn of the twentieth century, it may behoove us to re-evaluate the values that have helped the Tibetan people thrive for millennia. The ecological practices embraced by Tibetans have a parallel with our pressing global need to find a balance between our consumption and the earth's well-being.

The daunting challenges before us—including overpopulation, habitat destruction, ozone depletion, the greenhouse effect, and pollution—are all connected to destructive human activities. In our search for long-term, lasting solutions, cultures such as Tibet which have relied on a nature-based philosophy, remain important markers in our transition towards cooperation and coexistence among ourselves and with the environment. Our current crisis calls for creative approaches which protect diverse cultures that have successfully coexisted with the land.

It has been our intention in the development of this book to show the remarkable tenacity and ingenuity with which the Tibetan nomads and farmers have been able to thrive in this unique region of the world. We pay tribute to these rugged pastoralists and farmers who have acquired an earth-based wisdom. With a thorough knowledge of their environment, Tibetans have developed skills which have sustained them for generation after generation.

The material in *Tibet: Enduring Spirit, Exploited Land* is drawn from an oral history project completed by the authors and a team of dedicated Tibetans. We conducted a series of interviews with Tibetan refugees now living in India, Nepal, and the United States. The experiences described by former nomads and farmers illustrate a network of daily life on the Tibetan Plateau, providing an overview of the culture, the lifestyle of nomads and farmers from various regions of Tibet, and the relationship of Tibetans to their environment.

As we grapple with problems facing our entry into the next millennium, Tibetans stand like an endangered species whose survival is threatened by denuding their forest environment and eroding their soil and nutrients. By understanding the impact of our actions and inactions, and reversing the present trend, we can rebuild the soil, replenish the nutrients, and help the seeds to disperse and germinate. We hope that *Tibet: Enduring Spirit, Exploited Land* will help to spread this message, protect the roots of indigenous cultures, and revitalize the forest of our world community.

CHAPTER ONE

Ecology of the Land and People

"This close relationship between nature and our religion means the principles which maintain balance in the natural world have become a part of our daily lives. And after living like this for hundreds of years, it has become difficult for any Tibetan to differentiate between the practice of religion and concern for the environment."[1]

Tibetans came to understand ecological principles naturally. Their landscape had a will of its own, and the human beings who settled upon it were never permitted to lose sight of that fact. The wilderness could be fierce or friendly, generous or cruel. Survival meant unflagging attention and strict conservation, which Tibetans integrated into their religious rituals and every aspect of their lives. And since the vagaries of nature were perceived as the rumblings of the gods, all natural phenomena—even harmful ones—became opportunities for devotion. The fickle winds, which carried nourishing rain or violent storms, also whipped gossamer prayer flags that dispersed blessings over the landscape. Cold rivers, diverted for irrigation, drove paddle-powered prayer-wheels. All living things, from insects to yaks, were recognized as threads in this universal fabric, and all were deemed worthy of respect and protection.

Tibetans have no word for "ecology." Unlike Western civilization, which sought to tame the wild, the Tibetan people sought from earliest times to secure a kind of partnership with their wilderness. They never found the need to quantify the relationship between human beings and their environment. "We don't have the intellectual approach," observes Lama Kunga Rimpoche, the Tibetan monk who directs the

Ewam Choden Buddhist Center in Kensington, California. "Biology, psychology, zoology; we didn't have all those ologies. We did have our hearts and our feelings, and that developed an understanding that goes beyond words."

The notion that all paper products would be recycled—because to waste such resources would be an unbearable insult to the spirits of the trees and forests—seems quaintly naive to our Western sensibilities. So do the ideas that toxic wastes like motor oil and used mercury batteries should be disposed of diligently to avoid alienating the forces within the earth, that polluting streams and rivers is an unthinkable sacrilege, or that Tibetan farmers, mindful of their *karma*, shudder at the very thought of dusting crops with insecticide.

This spiritual view of the world is more than superstition. Only recently, our "sophisticated" society has come to accept the fact that a despoiled environment will rebel in one way or another; it is only a matter of time. Some scientists are starting to understand that the earth is a living, ever-changing organism capable of causing harm to those who fail to treat it with respect. Tibetans have understood these concepts for thousands of years.

By focusing on our immediate needs and failing to consider the interrelatedness of things, the industrialized world has brought the global environment frighteningly close to the breaking point. But as dire as our dilemma may be, it is not too late to effect change. Tibetans who spent over a millennium perfecting their wise ecological code have much to offer us—if we have the interest and patience to listen.

Western Tibet is a forbidding landscape—a realm of vast plains, ice-capped peaks, and scattered stones, sketched in bold mineral colors by the muscular arm of geology. Food is scarce. The people who inhabit this region subsist mainly on ground roasted barley *(tsampa)* with black tea, yak butter, and a bit of salt. Sometimes their diet is enlivened by yak meat, sometimes by a handful of dried cheese or some vegetables eked out of the miserly soil. Fresh fowl, one might think, would be a bounty for such people. It would not be surprising, therefore, to find hundreds of Tibetan villagers and nomads, armed with slings, bows, and primitive muskets, arriving by a lake where waterfowl nest every spring.

And arrive they did, but not to hunt. Hired by the district government and paid with local taxes, families set up tents by lake Lhamo Lhatso's shores with the express purpose of protecting the birds. The nomads and farmers kept a constant vigil, assuring that no predators, human or animal, threatened or disturbed the nesting creatures. Dogs and rodents, leopards and eagles, all were shooed away with stones and shouts until the waterfowl and their offspring began the long journey back to their winter homes.

The spirit of perpetual reverence that defined life in Tibet held sway in death as well. While wealthier families and lamas often chose to be cremated, most Tibetans disposed of their earthly remains in the ceremony of "sky burial." In this awesome ritual, the corpse was carried to a hilltop, carved into pieces, and then distributed to the birds and beasts; the ultimate act of recycling.

Tibetans placed very little importance on the concept of personal gain, at least as we view it in the West. The most eagerly sought boons were spiritual. Hiking a thousand miles to catch a glimpse of the Dalai Lama; prostrating for miles around the base of sacred Mount Kailas (See photo, pg. 33); raising enough money to sponsor a visiting lama—these were enviable achievements, and Tibetans would undergo extreme personal hardship to realize them.

This helps to explain why Tibet never invested its resources in developing technology—at least not in the mechanistic sense. Tibetologist Richard Kohn agrees with those who speak of traditional Tibet as similar to a medieval society, but argues that it is also a modern culture with an advanced psychological and spiritual "technology" that has evolved from Tibetan traditions. "The Tibetan technology is all inside," observes Kohn. "All their great inventions have to do with better ways to meditate, better ways to become a better human being—instead of inventing more entertaining video games, or better ways to reach Mars."[2] Khenpo Gyaltsen, a monk born in U-Tsang, agreed. "I think that in Tibet" he told us, "if no sophisticated technology was developed, it was because it was not needed. Everything that people needed was already there."

The unique aspects of Tibet's culture were described by Robert A. F. Thurman, professor of Buddhist studies at Columbia University and a former Buddhist monk who had lived in Tibet:

> [Tibet] is a culture of inestimable value to us, as a mirror image of ours, as extremely inward as we have been extremely outward. It may contain precious keys with which we can rediscover planetary equilibrium, restoring spiritual sanity to those maddened by extreme materialism. Its life or death is our life or death. It lives underground at home, in open air only in exile. We must protect it, nurture it and patiently wait for all concerned to rediscover its jewel-like value and need for special treasuring."[3]

The most remarkable thing about Tibetan culture is not the range of classes or regional costumes; it is how much all Tibetans held in common. The fundamental principles of caring for the land, of viewing environmental protection as an inseparable part of daily life, differed very little across Tibet's 1,500-mile breadth and rugged territory. As one sifts through the literature and speaks to individual Tibetans about their lives, these basic themes emerge again and again. Taken together, they form the foundation of Tibetan ecology, and explain why nearly all Tibetans—from the farmers of far eastern Amdo to the sheepskin-clad Rutok people of the west—have treated the land and its creatures with respect and forbearance.

The most basic teaching of the Buddha is exquisitely simple: All living beings endure hardship and all are worthy of respect and affection. Our actions toward other living creatures, the Buddha taught, determine our inner worth. Money, possessions, even our human bodies are transient. Only through diligent cultivation of our inner worth can we aspire to Buddhahood and release from the painful cycle of death and rebirth. Such teachings, with subtle differences, have been offered to humanity for thousands of years. In Tibet, however, they resonate with extraordinary power. The proscription against killing has permeated Tibetan society, informing every aspect of life and work. Yaks, it is true, are butchered for food, but only after the appropriate prayers, and with full awareness of the karmic implications.

To an outsider, the traditional Tibetan way of life may appear simple, even primitive. But behind this unpretentious lifestyle lies an elaborate network of laws, codes, and ethics—a complex philosophy whose roots reach back thousands of years to religious traditions that preceded even the arrival of Buddhism on the Tibetan Plateau.

An exiled abbot, the Venerable Lama Tashi Gyaltsen of the Dip Tse-Chok-Ling Tibetan Monastery School, said during an interview in Dharamsala, India: "When Buddhism came to Tibet…love, respect and compassion for all sentient beings definitely came to Tibet. I think there were many *Bodhisattvas*[4] before Buddha also. I think the respect for all land was there even before Buddhism was introduced to Tibet. [But] the way we perceived things may have been different then."

As is true of all Buddhists, Tibetans believe:

- The goal for all living beings is to attain enlightenment;

- All living beings go through a series of reincarnations along their path to enlightenment. Thus, in a previous life, we could have been anything from a single-cell organism to an insect or a dog, a poor starving leper or a prince or princess;

- Our condition in this life (and our previous and future lives) is dependent on a cycle of causes and effects called *karma*. Our actions determine *karma* and *karma* determines the conditions we endure.

- By "making merit" or performing good deeds, we can improve our *karma*.

Living in an area as large as Alaska, the Tibetan people were united by race, language, diet, and a common value system basic to their personal relationships. These values were an outgrowth of their Buddhist thought and beliefs.

A hallmark of Tibetan Buddhism is the belief that each individual must not only seek his or her own enlightenment, but that they should strive to help others attain it by helping to put an end to suffering. Thus, Tibetans attempt to always behave in an altruistic and compassionate manner.

When you consider the world in terms of "making merit," it is easy to understand why Buddhist monks and nuns—and even many lay Buddhists—adopt vows of *ahimsa*, or "non-harming," as a lifelong practice. Consideration for all living creatures is the most visible manifestation of the Buddhist faith and one which figures directly in the intimate equation linking Tibetans and their environment. Even though the strictest doctrine recommends that Buddhists not kill animals, including fish and fowl, and not eat their meat, the real-life hardships of life on the cold, dry Tibetan Plateau necessitated compromise.

Tibet was a theocracy where, from ancient times, religion played a central role in the traditional value structure. Its leaders—the Dalai Lamas and regents—composed a set of secular laws called *tsatsigs* in order to regulate these activities. These laws declared that animals could only be killed in certain numbers, and during certain seasons. Different provisions applied to different areas. Fishing, for example, might be permitted in a region of scarce wildlife, but prohibited among nomads with an abundant supply of yaks, even if a rich supply of fish darted through the streams that bordered their pastoral settlements.

Fishing was frowned upon because it involved taking many lives, whereas a single yak could feed a large number of people. M. H. Duncan, who explored Tibet extensively during the 1920s and 1930s, commented on the Tibetans' attitude toward killing fish: "After the cook selects our needs," he wrote, "our caravan leader, Drale Gonchoh, carefully carries the remainder back to liberty and life. Fish have no voice to protest their slaughter and it is more sinful to kill them [than] other animals."[5] Tibetans took these laws very seriously, treating them with the same respect as Buddhist directives.

We spoke with exiled abbot Tashi Gyaltsen, who lives in Dip Tse-Chok-Ling Monastery in Dharamsala. He grew up the son of a farmer and had a special appreciation for the wild animals that roamed near his birthplace at Kyirong, in western Tibet. He said of the region in Tibet where he had lived:

> It wasn't that we didn't have any meat—we did eat meat, but you rarely heard of someone killing an animal primarily for its meat—it was against the law of that region, and when we did eat meat it was from animals that had died either due to a natural cause

or by accident. For example, we might eat an animal that had fallen off a cliff, or was killed by a bear or a leopard. In our region, we were not allowed to kill even a bird.

The abbot also mentioned that at certain times of the year, no one in the region was allowed to kill or harm animals, lift stones, cut grass, or dig the soil.

In his book *Seven Years in Tibet*, Heinrich Harrer talks about the Tibetan attitude toward preserving life:

> After a short time in the country, it was no longer possible for one thoughtlessly to kill a fly, and I have never in the presence of a Tibetan squashed an insect which bothered me. The attitude of the people in these matters is really touching. If at a picnic an ant crawls up one's clothes, it is gently picked up and set down. It is a catastrophe when a fly falls into a cup of tea. It must at all cost be saved from drowning as it may be the reincarnation of one's dead grandmother.[6]

His Holiness the Fourteenth Dalai Lama states, "Our Tibetan culture, although highly influenced by Buddhism, did not gain all its philosophy from Buddhism.... People are always looking for answers in our unique religion, forgetting that our environment is just as unusual."[7] Tibetans never sought to master their landscape; that would have been futile. Instead, they developed a way to match their own rhythm of life with the larger rhythms of the seasons.

Living in Tibet, where the average altitude is nearly 15,000 feet, required the ability to compromise, accept limitations, and practice a lifestyle requiring conservation practices. Nothing was taken for granted; nothing was wasted. Tibetans did this so successfully for so long that the ecology of the region formed a foundation of their lifestyle.

Thus, a careful stewardship of Tibet's fragile ecology was maintained, while both material and spiritual needs were served. Tibetan refugees living in India told us that they had lived with these values all of their lives. For Tibetans, the environment was treated not as a force outside the human community, but as an integral aspect in all human endeavors. Nomads and farmers developed a sense of belonging to the environment and an awareness of their dependence on the natural world. They were aware that if they exploited their environment they were in essence exploiting and hurting themselves. The Tibetan attitude toward the environment fostered an atmosphere of cooperation rather than competition. In the Tibetan economic system, animals such as yaks, sheep, and goats represented personal wealth. However, the land, with its water and grazing rights, was shared by nomads and semi-nomads—a system markedly different from the Western practice of land ownership.

Tibetans used little wood for either fuel or building. They used yak dung for heating and cooking, and built mainly with mud and stone. Tibetans traditionally took care of their forests. For example, we were told by Alak Tsayi, a fifty-two-year-old monk from Tsayi in Amdo, that prior to 1950 "the forests in each region would be the property of the people of that region. If there were any forests near a monastery, they would be under the monastery's control. If one was near a village, the villagers would have authority over that forest.... [We were] told that if [we] cut a lot of trees, the value, the fertility of the land would finish off."

He went on to say, "You could not simply go and cut trees. If you wanted to construct a house or something, you had to write an application explaining why you needed the wood. The authorities would then see if you were really constructing a house, and then the permission to cut the trees would be granted. If you were not really building you would have to pay a fine."

The Tibetan respect for the environment helped to maintain an ecological equilibrium over a vast area. An example of the complex web of interrelationships required to maintain this ecological balance was described by M. H. Duncan:

> Some slopes are entirely barren, denuded by millions of mouse hares (Ochotona) who honeycomb the turf with countless tiny holes, connecting endless tunnels. Yellowish-brown steppe bears, light yellowish steppe foxes, golden-brown weasels, eagles and hawks keep. . . [the mouse hares] under control unless man destroys too many of their enemies. . . [Then the mouse hares eat] the grass roots to extinction and the rich barren

earth is left to the erosive power of water and wind so that both the simple nomad and the simpler mouse hares deprive themselves of food.[8]

The connection between the mouse hares, their predators, the weather, soil, vegetation, and human beings is part of a tightly woven web of systems and interactions that regulate each others' activities.

Slowly, the outside world is awakening to the value of Tibetan culture. The Land of Snows was virtually inaccessible a mere fifty years ago. Yet today, it is offered as a four-day stopover on packaged tours. Tibetan rituals are the subject of doctoral dissertations; Tibet's sacred art is displayed in huge, highly publicized exhibitions. Articles about Tibetan nomads appear in glossy national magazines, and the Dalai Lama—once the elusive "God-King of Tibet"—has won the Nobel Peace Prize and performed sacred initiations all over the world.

Tragically though, the past five decades have brought more than curious tour groups and well-meaning researchers to Tibet. They have also brought a wholesale invasion by the Peoples' Republic of China, which saw in Tibet's ore-streaked mountains, abundant forests, and open plains, a solution to its imminent scarcity of resources and its population increase.

Since the Chinese invasion and occupation of the 1950s, Tibet's fragile environment has been subject to crippling abuse. Vast tracts of forest in the lower reaches of the Brahmaputra and Mekong Rivers have been felled for Chinese mills, resulting in erosion and siltation so severe that they now threaten Asia's great waterways and the countries lying downstream to the south. Fertile croplands have been commandeered and leached of their nutrients by inappropriate, government-dictated farming practices. Wild animals, protected for centuries by religious laws, have been slaughtered by the tens of thousands.

Meanwhile, Tibet's human population, at one with the environment, has been persecuted, intimidated, and pushed aside by Han Chinese settlers. Since the forced annexation, more than 1.2 million Tibetans have been shot by Chinese troops or have died in prisons and forced labor camps. The International Commission of Jurists has reported the occupation as a prima facie case of genocide. Countless other Tibetans starved to death when farmers, traditionally geared toward barley cultivation, were forced to grow wheat, with little success. The Chinese demolished Tibet's monastery system, destroying more than 6,000 monasteries—but not before their sacred artworks were removed and either melted down for shipment to Beijing or sold on the black market. By 1966, fewer than 7,000 of Tibet's 115,000 monks and nuns remained.

The most serious long-term threat is Chinese population transfer. Lured by huge government-supported economic bonuses and ever bleaker prospects in China proper, millions of Chinese are being relocated all over Tibet. Within the shrunken boundaries of what is now called the Tibetan Autonomous Region, Chinese already outnumber Tibetans. In Lhasa, the ratio is three-to-one. The population transfer policy spells disaster for Tibetans, their culture, and their way of life. More than 120,000 Tibetans, including the Dalai Lama, have already been forced to flee their homeland. Unless the Chinese relent, Tibetan exiles all over the world may live to see the day when their sacred landscape and ancient culture are completely overwhelmed.

Tibetan attitudes and practices raise important questions for the industrialized world. We are challenged to understand their voices and find ways to apply their wisdom to our world. The Tibetan people represent a "seed culture" whose value structure may help us redefine our own beliefs regarding resource management, technology, and community. The Tibetan "seeds" include the knowledge of ecological practices that have been a part of their culture for thousands of years. In keeping with the tenets of Tibetan Buddhism, which place the highest value on education, service, and generosity, we hope that *Tibet: Enduring Spirit, Exploited Land* will help to inform the modern world about ecological practices that can be a source of learning for the present and the future.

And if this gift is of use to us in the West, perhaps we can find a way to repay the favor with an earnest effort, supported by the community of free nations, to help restore the stewardship of Tibet to the Tibetans. For even though Tibet will never again be what it once was—a forbidden, mysterious realm guarded by snowy, sentinel peaks—it may in fact become something more. It is the dream of the Dalai Lama, shared by nearly every Tibetan, to see the Land of Snows evolve into a vast geographic zone of peace, an international wildlife sanctuary, and a global tribute to the ideals of wisdom and compassion.

NOTES

1. Tenzin Atisha, "The Tibetan Approach to Ecology," *The Anguish of Tibet*, ed. Petra K. Kelly, Gert Bastian, and Pat Aiello (Berkeley: Parallax Press, 1991): 222–23.
2. Taken from an interview with Richard Kohn, Tibetologist.
3. Robert A. F. Thurman, "An Outline of Tibetan Culture," CS *Quarterly* 12, no. 1: 66.
4. A Bodhisattva is an enlightened individual who chooses not to enter nirvana in hopes of helping others attain enlightenment.
5. M. H. Duncan, *Yangtze and the Yak*. (Ann Arbor, Mich.: Edwards Brothers, 1952), 81.
6. Heinrich, Harrer, *Seven Years in Tibet* (New York: Jeremy P. Tarcher/ Perigee Books, Putnam Publishing Group, 1981), 178–79, 191.
7. Tenzin Gyatso, the Fourteenth Dalai Lama of Tibet, and Galen Rowell, My *Tibet* (Berkeley and Los Angeles: University of California Press, 1990), 79.
8. M. H. Duncan, *The Yangtze and the Yak* (Alexandria, Va.: Merchant Press, 1952), 75.

CHAPTER TWO

The Geography of the Land of Snows

"Reports from Western observers who visited Tibet earlier in this century, before the Chinese occupation, emphasized the spiritual quality of the Tibetans' relationship to their land and their profound sense of the interdependence of life forms. Their Buddhism had one of the clearest expression in the care with which they husbanded their natural resources."[1]

Many people who visualize Tibet imagine a desolate, snow-blown, spiritual land, broken by impossible peaks and punctuated by lonely monasteries: The "Land of Snows." These notions about Tibet reflect the longings and aspirations of travelers and authors who wrote about their visits to Tibet, starting in the eighteenth century. These early images have been built and elaborated upon by subsequent expeditions over the years to the point that they are firmly fixed in the Western psyche.

Unfortunately, distorted images of Tibet still remain in the minds of many, influenced by the exploits of explorer Sir Edmund Hillary, the first Westerner to climb Mt. Everest, and James Hilton's utopian vision of Shangri-La. These images need to be recognized, one as honoring heroism, the other reflecting the desire for nirvana. As one writer notes, "Tibet became a landscape to which the soulful imaginings of many Westerners were drawn, one which has sustained deep fascination over the centuries."[2]

Though much of Tibet matches the imaginings of a foreboding landscape, especially in winter, visitors are often astonished to find in various parts of Tibet lush forests teeming with birds, rolling meadows carpeted with wildflowers, and vast plains waving with iridescent fields of barley, mustard, and emerald alpine grass. In the past, the wildlife was so abundant that these areas were likened to the plains in Africa, where large herds of animals roamed. It is no wonder that a land approximately the size of Alaska, with a varied array of ecological niches, would possess such diversity (See photos, pp. 35,39).

Tibet's dramatic geological history—as the point of tectonic plate impact between the Indian subcontinent and the Eurasian land mass—created zones of prodigious variety, and a kind of natural sanctuary for hundreds of indigenous plant species and dozens of native animals. Orchids and rhododendrons bloom in the Himalayan foothills, sheltered from the cold by alpine trees and shrubs (See photo, pg. 34). Even banana trees and other tropical plants flourish in the lower zones, near the Brahmaputra River and only a few hundred miles east of Mt. Everest. This river's course forms the world's largest and deepest canyon, exceeding the depth and length of the Grand Canyon. Reaching depths of 16,000-feet, it was cut two million years ago during the Pliocene Epoch. Because of its remoteness and depth, the canyon has yet to be fully explored.

Visions from an Earlier Time

The first Western explorers, many of them scientists, visited Tibet in the late 1800s and during the first half of the twentieth century. They were amazed by the country's biodiversity. The vast variety of flora and fauna included monkeys, wild asses, and red pandas roaming the lower forests, while at the higher reaches blue sheep, snow leopards, and wild yaks were commonplace. Over five hundred species of birds were spotted in Tibet, from tiny finches to the enormous lamergeier, whose nine-foot wingspan enables it to hover over ice-capped pinnacles like a pterodactyl.

Today, most visitors fly into Tibet from Nepal or China. The first scene to catch their eye is the drab landing strip and concrete housing at the airport, some hours distance from the capital at Lhasa. Those traveling to Tibet just four decades ago journeyed by foot and horse through the ever-changing landscape into the interior. Lama Govinda, a European-born Buddhist monk, described his impressions as he traveled through Sikkim, up the Chumbi Valley into Central Tibet, in the mid-1940s:

The journey had a dream-like quality: rain, fog, clouds transformed the virgin forest, the rocks and mountains, gorges and precipices into a world of uncannily changing, fantastic forms, which appeared and dissolved with such suddenness that one began to doubt their reality as well as one's own. Mighty waterfalls hurled from invisible heights into an equally invisible bottomless depth. Clouds above and clouds below the narrow path, surging up and sinking again, revealing views of breathtaking grandeur for one moment and blotting them out in the next.

Trees appeared like many-armed giants with long gray beards of moss, entangled in creepers and festooned with delicate light green garlands that swung from tree to tree.... In the lower altitudes blossoming orchids and ferns sprouted from tree-trunks and branches. Clouds, rocks, trees, and waterfalls created a fairyland worthy of the imagination of a romantic Chinese landscape painter, and the small caravan of men and horses moved through it like miniature figures in a vast landscape scroll....

The ascent seemed to have no end—indeed, even the sky was no more the limit!—and each stage revealed a new type of landscape, climate and vegetation. The exuberant, moist-warm, leech-infested, fever-laden tropical virgin forest...gave way to the more sober forest of subtropical and temperate zones . . .[3]

Describing the reaches beyond the more florid regions, he wrote:

Soon these were left behind, and we entered the near-arctic zone, in which only stunted fir and dwarf rhododendron...could survive in a world of titanic rock, snow-covered peaks among which low-hanging clouds and sudden burst of sunshine created a constantly changing play of light and shadow. What was here a minute ago had disappeared in the next.

And then the great miracle...on the highest point of the pass the clouds that in huge masses surged angrily and threateningly dark against the mountain wall, dissolved into thin air as if by magic, the gates of heaven were opened and a world of luminous colors under a deep blue sky stretched before one's eyes and a fierce sun lit up the snow-covered slopes on the other side of the pass so that one was almost blinded by their brilliance...[4]

Even today, if travelers could avoid seeing the extensively deforested areas, landslides, and silted-up rivers, they would be left with the awe Lama Govinda described. But explorers, scientists, and adventurers of the past described and documented a Tibet that essentially no longer exists today. Peter Bishop, commenting in 1989 about earlier descriptions of Tibet, stated:

> The place of Tibet had a logic, a coherence of its own, its genius loci. Tibet was not a "silent other," it was alive, substantial and compelling. It was part of the world calling attention to itself, deepening our soulful appreciation of mountains, of deserts and rivers, of light and colour, of time and space, of the myriad peoples and their cultures, of fauna and flora, of the plurality of imaginative possibilities.[5]

Geographic Diversity

With the advent of modern transport, today few travelers, with the exception of the hardiest trekkers and the most devout pilgrims, are exposed to the experience of traversing Tibet's varied and unique ecological niches. Although Tibet is ecologically unique, it does not appear alien. If you were to walk across the countryside, parts of it might remind you of the more arid and desolate regions of Montana and Wyoming. Some of the rainforests would appear similar to those on the Olympic Peninsula in the state of Washington. The Tibetan prairies would remind one of vast stretches of open land in northern Canada.

Seen by an astronaut from the high altitude of a space ship, the land mass that has been called The Land of Snows looks like a giant boulder situated in the surrounding flatness of the neighboring regions of India and China. Of special significance to all of Asia are the rivers that arise in the highlands of Tibet. In the region of Mt. Kailas in western Tibet, all the major rivers of Asia—the Indus, the Yangtse, Yellow, Brahmaputra, Mekong, Irrawadi, and the Salween—begin their journey to the sea. The health and well-being of Pakistan, India, Burma, Thailand, Cambodia, and Vietnam, as well as much of China, depend upon the health of these rivers. Indiscriminate deforestation, mining, and atomic waste dumping in Tibet can lead to climate changes and flooding as well as catastrophic levels of soil and water contamination in every nation that depends upon the water and topsoil carried by these rivers.

Each of the three major political regions of Tibet—the Northern Plain (U-Tsang), Southern Tibet (Kham), and Eastern Tibet (Amdo)—include three or more distinct climatic and vegetation zones, ranging from less than 3,000 feet to over 29,000 feet above sea level (See map, Appendix E). Grasslands and rangelands cover almost 70 percent of Tibet's total area. While the grasslands take up the majority of Tibet's productive land and are home to a half million nomads, farmlands occupy a mere 2 percent of the country. Farms are found mainly in small niches of valley bottoms in all three regions. The areas are extremely fertile and produce much of the barley needed for the Tibetan diet, plus surplus that can be traded for other household needs.

In the past, trails rather than roads were the typical byways in Tibet. A system of roads to travel from place to place was developed only recently. The nomads still use the yak as a beast of burden for transporting their households. The horse, the nomad's most valuable possession, has been the typical mode of travel.

The Northern Plain (U-Tsang)

The Northern Plain is the largest region of the country. This vast area called the Changthang, covers a large portion of the country. To the extreme north is a cold, desolate desert quarter neighboring on the Chinese-Turkestan border that is mostly uninhabited. The western part of this region, which borders on Ladakh, supports a small number of nomads who live off the scant vegetation. In the 1950s, U-Tsang was sectioned off by the Chinese and named the Tibetan Autonomous Region (TAR) (See photo, pg. 37).

The southern part of the Changthang is a mostly dry plateau, corrugated with snow-covered peaks, sparsely covered valleys, and pristine lakes. There is a great deal of thermal activity underground to the north of Lhasa, where many areas fume with steam holes and geysers (See photo, pg. 69). The high Himalayas act as a barrier to the rain, keeping much of the moisture from reaching this vast region. Because of the extreme climate and altitude, on the average 14,500 feet, there is little forest here. However, some rain does cross over the mountains in the spring and summer, usually enough to turn the plains into a rich, grassy, grazing region that supports a half-million nomads with their herds of yak, sheep, and goats.

This is the historic realm of the birthplace of the Tibetan nation, where the ancestors of the present Tibetans evolved a unique and sustainable way of life in which nature and man became harmoniously inseparable. With its high altitude and dry, piercing cold climate, it is one of most physically demanding regions where man has managed to thrive. Traveling through it, one is impressed by a vision of sky, mountains, plains, and lakes. The human presence with the yaks, horses, sheep, and goats, blends into the landscape; everything seems an element in the natural order of things, with nothing out of place. The three largest cities in this region, Lhasa, Gyanze, and Shigatse, are situated in broad, fertile valleys where there is extensive farming. Lhasa, the ancient capital of Tibet, is located along the Kyi Chu River, where the massive monastery-fortress of the Potala rises, majestically dominating the surrounding country side.

Southern Tibet (Kham)

In southern Tibet (Kham), the Bramhaputra, Mekong, Salween, and Yangtse rivers rush through deep valleys on their lengthy journey through Bangladesh, India, and Southeast Asia, flowing into the Bay of Bengal, the Cambodian Sea, and the China Sea. These rivers irrigate most of the rice-growing areas of Southeast Asia. Kham receives the heaviest rainfall in Tibet (See photo, pg. 36).

On a map, this area looks pleated like an accordion. The region's mountain ranges run hundreds of miles in an almost parallel pattern, providing pathways for the raging rivers through deep, heavily forested gorges. They descend from over 20,000 feet down to less than 3,000 feet. Commencing on the grassy high plateau, they descend through great coniferous forests to the lowest altitudes in Tibet, flowing through subtropical growth until they reach the sea. Of all of Tibet, this area is the most difficult to reach, and sections are not yet fully explored.

The people of Kham live in a variety of scattered niches in this mountainous region, ranging from small fertile enclaves in the lower valleys, where they practice subsistence agriculture, to upland meadows, where they are more dependent upon a nomadic existence, tending yak, sheep, and goats for their livelihood. Like the nomads in the Changthang, the Khampa nomads move their tent sites up and down the mountainside, in order to graze their animals on the new growth in the pastures. During our interviews with nomads, one elderly man from Kham told us, "In the winter it is very cold and almost all the time it is windy and the wind carries lots of dust. In the summertime when the weather becomes pleasant, flowers grow in such abundance it appears as if a rainbow fell to earth."

In this part of Tibet grew the greatest forests, which are now steadily being denuded by the Chinese. The hillsides are becoming increasingly barren. The hastily built lumbering roads have produced large landslides and the silting of rivers, which is having a devastating effect on the valleys and plains to the south (See Chapter 5).

Eastern Tibet (Amdo)

Eastern Tibet (Amdo) combines many of the features of northern and southern Tibet. The altitude ranges from 16,000 feet to approximately 3,000 feet. Amdo accounts for about 30 percent of the total land traditionally inhabited by Tibetan-speaking people. In the high mountains and steep valleys to the north, the rainfall is more plentiful than in the TAR. Large stretches of extremely fertile grasslands exist here, so the nomads can graze their yaks and other livestock with relative ease. The vastness of the grass ranges have been the pride of the various Tibetan tribal groups long inhabiting this region (See photo, pg. 38).

M. H. Duncan, who explored this region of Tibet for fifteen years starting in the 1920s, noted that the thousands of yak that grazed there "are unable to consume but a fraction of the succulent grass." He anticipated "a time when the number of yak can be increased until the Tibetan Tableland becomes the last great reservoir of beef to supply a crowded world."[6] Duncan's predictions didn't foresee the disruption in the ecological balance that now has brought hardship to this land. To the east and the south lie extensive, dense evergreen forests covering about 18 percent of the province. These forests are more accessible than those in Kham, and in recent years they also have been extensively denuded, falling prey to dynamite, the chain saw, and ax of the occupying Chinese. The wealth of the forest in this region was described by M. H. Duncan:

> We pitch our tents amid magnificent trees; god-maples three feet in diameter and a hundred feet high, five-leafed poplar maples, golden oak, spruce, pines, holly oak, juniper and red firs, these last being over three feet in diameter and 150 feet in the air. A few homes are tucked in open spaces among the giant trees whose quietness and mystery charmed us. It is 11,600 feet above the sea level. . . .
>
> We surmount a low pass and slide easily onto the western end of an immense tussocked plain five to ten miles wide which trends northwest and southeast for a length of twenty to thirty miles. Upon it roam vast herds of wild ass [the Tibetan *kyang*] in groups, as I count them, often 500 to 1,000.[7]

Because of the abundant rainfall in the deepest valleys of this region, the growth varies from subalpine to subtropical, allowing the inhabitants to grow multiple crops each year.

Living along a permeable boundary with China, the Tibetans in Amdo, as in Kham, have struggled to maintain their separate identities. Historically, these border areas have also been populated by Chinese, Uigurs, and other minority groups. The Goloks of Amdo, horsemen living in the extensive grasslands of Amdo, stand out as perhaps the most independent of the Tibetans. While maintaining their distance from other groups in their area, they still have a strong identity as Tibetans.

The availability of the fertile areas where intense farming can be carried out differs considerably in the three provinces. Changthang has the most land for grazing. In Kham, one will find the richest river bottom land for lucrative multicrop growing. With the great differences in the fertility of the land, it is natural to find variations in lifestyles. The bulk of Tibetans in Kham are agrarian folk who farm or graze livestock. These rural Tibetans characterize themselves as either farmers, semi-nomads *(samarogs)*, or as nomads *(drokpas)*.

The semi-nomads maintain permanent residences as do the farmers, but in the spring when the grasses on the slopes become abundant, they leave their farms, taking their families, tents, and livestock with them to the rich grazing areas. The farmers generally live much closer to the villages and small towns and have greater access to essential resources for living.

Natural Resources of Tibet

Traditionally, the Tibetans have been very protective of their forest, and no trees were felled unless essential for building. Herbs and medicinal plants have been gathered and used as part of both Tibetan and Chinese medicine. There were always enough herb-producing plants in Tibet to allow for natural replenishment. Whatever riches there were underneath the soil were left as part of nature's grand design —it is not the Tibetan way to dig for riches under the soil. Tibetans were thankful to the earth for what it provided them above the ground.

Historically, in Tibet as a whole, notwithstanding the vast desert areas and untamable mountains, there was an abundance of products of nature to sustain the Tibetan people indefinitely. Their society was built on a conservation ethic, with waste being kept to a minimum. Through the traditional barter system between the nomadic people and farmers, there was enough food to satisfy Tibet's small population of approximately six million inhabitants. Variations in their diet are due to the accessibility of various foods in different areas.

Pradyumma P. Karam, in *The Changing Face of Tibet,* wrote, "The Tibetan landscape possessed supernatural significance, and economic activities such as farming served not only as a means of subsistence, but as a form of participation in religious life." The land and the creatures that roamed on it were a part of the Tibetan's world view which respects all forms of existence.[8]

The Tibetans' characteristics of kindheartedness, generosity, and human warmth are a direct outgrowth of their Buddhist thoughts and beliefs. While in continuous contact with the Han Chinese living at their borders over the millennia, they borrowed an insignificant amount of Chinese culture. But with the increasing presence of the Chinese throughout Tibet since the 1950s, much has been done to transform Tibet, Tibetan culture, and the tranquillity once associated with it.

NOTES

1. Sub-Commission of the United Nations on Prevention of Discrimination and Protection of Minorities, July 14, 1992.
2. Peter Bishop, *The Myth of Shangri-la: Tibet; Travel Writing and the Western Creation of the Sacred Landscape* (Berkeley: University of California Press, 1989), 6.
3. Lama Govinda, *The Way of the White Cloud* (London: Hutchinson, 1969), 41.
4. Ibid., 42.
5. Peter Bishop, *The Myth of Shangri-la,* 251.
6. M. H. Duncan, *The Yangtze and the Yak* (Alexandria, Va.: Merchant Press, 1952), 74.
7. Ibid., 77.
8. Pradyumna P. Karam, *The Changing Face of Tibet* (Lexington: University of Kentucky Press, 1976), 2.

CHAPTER THREE

The Nomadic Way of Life

"The personality attributes of the ideal pastoralist may be summarized as follows: a high degree of independence for action; a willingness to take chance; a readiness to act, and a capacity for action, self-containment and control, especially in the face of danger…and a realistic appraisal of the world."[1]

While nearly 85 percent of Tibet's rural population relied on the country's limited supply of arable land, the remaining 15 percent exploited the high, seemingly infinite wilderness that typified the majority of Tibet's surface area. These nomads, or *drokpa*, migrated through the inhospitable plains of the northern and central plateaus, clinging to a lifestyle that was born before the first Tibetan ruler was enthroned in 247 B.C. Herding huge flocks of yak and sheep, these self-sufficient and independent people thrived at an average altitude of 15,000 feet. Existing in this rarefied air, they possessed an almost supernatural sensitivity to the slightest nuances of their environment. The flavor of the wind and the color of the sparse tundra grasses provided critical clues to solving the continuing puzzle of how to survive on the roof of the world (See photos, pp. 45, 47).

Nomad life was perfectly attuned to the rhythms of the seasons. During the spring, the nomads would rise for their daily chores at dawn and begin by milking their goats and sheep—the goats' milk would be drunk and the sheep's milk would be used in making cheese and butter. When the milking was finished, the animals, including yaks, would be free to graze until herded back by the children in the late afternoon. In the summer, milking would be done twice, the animals being herded back by early morning and again by late afternoon. As the days grew longer and warmer, the herders drove their flocks ever higher, letting them graze on new growth in broad meadows (sometimes as high as 17,500 feet). By early evening, the yaks would be back in their encampment. After supper, the family would prepare for the next day.

By fall, the grasses were plentiful, and it was not uncommon for a group of nomads to camp a full month in the same pasture. As the days grew shorter and cooler, the sheep's milk would run dry, and only the goats and *dzo* (yak-cattle hybrid) would be milked (See photo, pg. 48). The seasonal variation of the quality of cheese (curd) was described by Nimgma, a nomad from the Nepal border region: "In the summer and spring the curd from the milk is not very delicious and is very watery. In the autumn, the curd prepared from goat's milk is very tasty." After milking, there would be time for weaving tent material, clothes, and making bags for carrying loads on yaks and sheep. As winter approached, the encampments would be arranged with tents set up in clusters. Important tasks centered around taking care of the animals and collecting dung for cooking and for keeping the fire going to brace against the freezing weather. The diet was restricted mostly to meat, milk, cheese, and *tsampa* (roasted barley) (See photo, pg. 40).

Nomads traditionally recognized their yaks and the land as the source of their wealth and well-being. Their yaks represented a livelihood which provided them with food, shelter, heat, clothing, transportation, and a range of other amenities that helped them thrive in the harsh Tibetan Plateau. In describing the yak, Nimgma told us: "[The] yak is a very useful animal. It helps in transportation and carrying any amount of load. It is the beast of burden. The yak helps in crossing rivers, climbing mountains, going any long distance. It helps in fetching salts from the north, going on business trips carrying loads to the south, carrying loads while shifting camps.... Its hide is useful in making ropes, tents, shoes.... Our tents are very warm and far better than any ordinary house. It also provides us with meat.... We get milk from dri [female yak]...it's very tasty" (See photos, pp. 66,67).

Yaks, in turn, were dependent on the healthy management of pasture lands, which were guarded against overgrazing. Nomads were keenly aware of the carrying capacity, or the number of animals the land could sustain. Palden, who lived in Kham, is a Tibetan man in his sixties who grew up in a family he considered wealthy. Since his family owned land as well as animals, they lived as semi-nomads, and there were several servants living with the family. Palden spoke about pasturing animals: "We would route our animals to other pastures when little grass was left," he said. "In the next season, good grass will grow, provided there is good rainfall. Then grass grows so abundantly that not only do the animals have enough to eat, but even the people will have enough grass to carry back home." The extra grass was used to supplement the diet of horses owned by wealthier families. The Tibetans' management of their animals, along with the climate and their pasturing practices, created an interdependent relationship that benefited the people as well as the environment.

When winter came, the *drokpas* returned to their winter camps in the lower valleys. Most nomads pitched their yak-hair dwellings close together to form a circle of tents, sheltered from the wind by walls made of stone and dried yak dung. The nomad existence was marked by severe weather, the constant threat of scarcity, and spartan living conditions. In such an unforgiving environment, waste was inconceivable. Hide and hair, dung and sinew, horns and stones, all found their best and highest use in the nomad encampments, becoming the raw material of tents, shoes, clothing, rope, windbreaks, and cooking fires. Being experienced in dealing with the vagaries of nature in this region, the nomads became high-altitude specialists. Their ingenuity and expertise were revealed in myriad ways: from the pasture-book system, which assured an equitable division of grasslands, to their prowess with the simplest tools and materials made from bone or stone.

Under the pasture-book system, the land, which was primarily owned by aristocrats or monasteries, was divided into specific parcels assigned to particular nomad families. In return for use of the land, nomads paid their landlord in wool, meat, and butter. This system allowed Tibetan nomads to follow well-developed itineraries through the grasslands during the brief growing season, while remaining in a more or less permanent encampment during the rest of the year.

Traveling in the U-Tsang, a visitor could watch in amazement as eight-year-old nomad boys fitted stones into hand-woven yak-hair slings. The slings were whipped until they whistled and the stones flew out with loud cracks. Seconds later, on the flanks of distant hillsides, errant yaks leaped into the air and returned to their herds. But sometimes young children forgot their duties and had to pay the consequences. "At our encampment, there were many wolves and leopards," recalled one former semi-nomad from Kham. Jamyang, who is now seventy-four and living in exile in India, continued speaking of his childhood: "I didn't see many tigers. These animals were very harmful to the animals under our care. When we were sent with our sheep to the mountains, we would busy ourselves playing with other children. Sometimes we saw eagles, crows, and other birds floating in the sky. [Their presence was a clue] that wolves had killed two or three of our sheep. When we came home in the evening, we were in real trouble…our parents punished us.… Some bad people killed [predatory] animals, but because our people were Buddhist, they didn't kill the foxes and wolves, even if they attacked our domestic animals."

Dogs, huge Tibetan mastiffs, were used to protect "the sheep during night time," explained Norbu, a former semi-nomad from Amdo who became a monk before he fled to India. "The mastiffs were very dangerous," he said. "They never bit or attacked [their] master[s], but a strong young man could not fight off a mastiff. Mastiffs went around the sheep at night and protected them from being attacked by wolves. The sheep didn't move until we took them to new pastures the next day."

Tibetan nomad children learned about rearing yaks, making cheese and butter, and conserving fuel by working hand-in-hand with their parents and siblings to take care of their household chores. Children also learned about weather patterns, grasslands, and the location and behavior of local wildlife. This knowledge gave nomad children a basic understanding of the workings of the ecological systems that were the source of their livelihood (See photos, pp. 71–73).

Tibetans loved their animals. Purba, who had been a semi-nomad, described the female yak as being "like one's mother," because they were so dependent on the yak as a source of well-being. Tibetans often regarded their animals as special pets. "I had a sheep," said Purba. "I had him from the time he was a lamb. My parents told me he and I were born on the same day. He had real big horns and his name was Karma. Well, I really liked him a lot. I would give him *momos* and *tsampa* (my favorite foods), as much and whenever I could. He had really grown fat. If I called him, 'Karma! Karma!,' he would come running even if he was very far away. And I would give him food, even if there wasn't enough for me. When I was small I didn't want him killed, so I saved his life. He lived almost twenty years and died of old age." The Chinese imprisoned Purba because he protested the jailing of his brother. Now forty-four, he had fled to India after he and his wife, whom he met in prison, were set free in 1987.

It was the yak, of course, that was the symbol and lifeblood of nomads throughout Tibet. "My parents were nomads," said Nawang Khechog, a Tibetan flautist from Kham who recently settled in New York City. "They had yaks and sheep; they herded and milked them. But the yak was most useful. Our tent was made from strong hair of the yak; we cooked the bones, and ate and drank the yak's milk, cheese, meat and butter. All these things. Without the yak, I don't think the nomads could survive."

"Nomads cut the yak hair only once yearly in the summer months," explained Norbu, the former nomad from Amdo who had become a monk. "When the yak hair got wet in the rain and you left it for many days, it never got rotten. The shorter hair of the yak, which in Tibetan is referred to as *khulu,* is smooth and warm like cotton when you make a mattress from it. The long yak hair is not smooth—it's rough and very strong when you make thread out of it. A tent made out of the best yak hair is waterproof when it rains. Some nomad [women] made a few rolls of woven yak hair a day. Then the next day, they did the same amount. Within a year they had enough to make a new tent when the old tent siding needed to be replaced." Norbu, who had escaped to India from the Drepung Monastery in 1959, added that some men gathered the wool by pulling it from the yak's body, rather than cutting it. They did this, he said, because they believed the hair would be stronger when gathered this way. But Norbu said he believed it was bad karma to pull the hair out, because it caused the animals pain. Yak hair was also used for sewing shoe soles, because it did not rot, and for making bags to store dried cheese.

"Tibetans are grateful to the yak," said Tashi, a semi-nomad who fled to India from northern Tibet. "Normally, yaks live for twenty or thirty years. Many families never slaughter their yaks when they get old. [These people] just allow them to die a natural death."

Tibetan nomads mastered the ability to live with the whims of nature. The nomads knew that, in their harsh land where severe weather and threat of scarcity were realities, they had to plan carefully for less abundant times. Using nature's own refrigeration process, the nomads preserved meat (which can stay frozen for most of the year) and cheese for the bad times they anticipated would be ahead. This conservation strategy enabled the *drokpa* to bridge those periods from year to year when shortages came.[2]

Living the life of a semi-nomad along the Khagyn Yungu River, Norbu and his family grew crops and tended yaks. As a young man, he joined the Labrang monastery and became a monk. Although he left Tibet for India while still young, he has an impressive knowledge of Tibetan plants and wildlife. Before he joined the monastery, his life as a semi-nomad was typical. In winter, he told us, "The valleys and mountains become white and the streams are covered by ice and sometimes we have difficulty getting drinking water. So we have to melt ice. Whenever the nomads want to cook food, they have to melt either snow or ice for water. The domestic animals have to lick the ice or they have to eat snow. If it becomes sunny after a snowfall, on the sunny side of the valley you can sometimes get some water." The winter snows confer an advantage later in the year. "Because of the heavy snow in winter," Norbu said, "we have very good grass in the summer."

Although yaks were the keystone of the nomadic economy, goats and sheep also provided an important addition to the nomad's food supply and wealth. Goats and sheep were not as dependable as the yak, however, because they were more vulnerable to weather conditions and more likely to be killed by wild animals. To protect them from predators, nomads used different schedules for putting goats and sheep out to graze than they did for yaks. Nomad families needed to own a large number of animals in order to maintain health and household. As we have seen, the animals were needed as a source of day-to-day food and as a source of other animal by-products. But they also represented the family treasure. (See photos, pp. 43, 44, 68)

When asked what was most important for the prosperity of the nomads, Nimgma, a nomad from the Nepal border region, told us: "Our prime concern is to increase the livestock. All the nomads will be working towards improving and increasing the livestock. In this matter, the father and the mother have a special role in guiding the other members of the family and servants to take maximum care of the animals. They should be taken to the best pastures and should be well looked after.... In such a case [the female yak] will give not only good milk, but also high quality wool which is whiter and longer." Speaking of common problems that afflict the animals, he said, "Some sheep would get infested with lice that would stop the proper growth of wool. Similarly, there are diseases common with the yaks; they should be prevented. . . ." Nomads tried to keep as many animals as possible, because when the whims of nature and fortune befell them, animals could be traded for other needed items. During the winter, the families would build stone or mud walls to protect the animals and their encampment from the wind, and would return to these sites in succeeding seasons (See photo, p. 68).

When they moved, Tibetan nomads tended to migrate only short distances—often not more than forty miles at a time, moving both vertically and horizontally as they traveled along the steep contours of their land. These migrations took advantage of the best pastures and improved yield by allowing the nomads to leave some fields fallow in a given year to enrich the soil.

At the end of the growing season, when the grasses were eaten to the ground, the nomads drove the animals to lower areas. The transition to lower and more permanent sites, often a drop of three thousand feet, made life during the coldest periods of winter more bearable for both the nomads and their animals. Even at the lower altitudes, however, the rivers could remain frozen for many months, leaving the nomads without a source of water. In spite of the extreme cold, the Changthang during winter,

North face of Mt. Kailas, 22,028 feet, in western Tibet (U-Tsang).
One of the most sacred sites in Tibet, Mt. Kailas has for
centuries been the object of pilgrimages.

Rhododendrons in the Kama Valley, east of Mt. Everest (U-Tsang). Wooded habitats add to the diversity of Tibet's landscape where vegetation adapts to varying elevations.

Oracle lake, a sacred site for Tibetans (U-Tsang). Many such lakes are said to provide visions for the future of Tibetans and their homeland.

Yarlung Valley, with ruins of an ancient monastery destroyed by the Chinese. This region gave birth to Tibet's first king, Nyatri Tsenpo in 127 B.C., and the Yarlung Dynasty which lasted 1,000 years (Kham).

Mt. Guarisankar, 21,000 feet (U-Tsang). Tibetan nomads have traditionally grazed sheep on plateaus such as these. Since the occupation, with the influx of Chinese settlers, the nomads have generally been forced to higher and less desirable pasture lands.

Rich pasture land in Amdo. Much of the fertile soil of this region in northeastern Tibet has been settled by the Chinese.

Stream with lush vegetation in an upper valley (U-Tsang). The Tibetans we interviewed described how the Chinese put in road systems, and many of these pristine, isolated areas have become subject to resource exploitation.

A nomadic woman grinding barley in an encampment east of Lhasa (U-Tsang). The ground barley is traditionally roasted for "*tsampa*," a staple in the Tibetan diet.

Two people from Kham, traveling across Tibet on a pilgrimage to sacred Mt. Kailas, pause to prepare yak-butter tea. Pilgrimage was once an integral part of life and the fondest dream of Tibetans of all classes. The Chinese campaign to suppress Buddhism and loyalty to the Dalai Lama has discouraged pilgrimages.

Khampa nomads preparing the midday meal (Kham).

Livestock huddled together for warmth during the cold, windy days of winter. Limits imposed by the Chinese government on herd sizes and trading and grazing practices have disrupted the nomads' livelihood.

Nomads who have ammassed sheep must be vigilant for predators when camping in exposed areas (U-Tsang).

A yak caravan traversing the Tingri Valley (U-Tsang). Ruins of a monastery loom in the background. Nomads traditionally traveled for days to barter their goods in village markets.

Nomads take time from their daily chores to socialize, a valued pastime.

A nomad encampment subject to unpredictable weather in a wind-swept valley (U-Tsang).

Nomads' goats are tied together in long rows to keep them from straying during milking (U-Tsang).

with its cobalt blue sky and rarefied air, is among the sunniest places in the world. The difference between the high temperatures of day and the cold of night is great—as much as a temperature drop of 80 degrees Fahrenheit.

With the Himalayas creating a formidable barrier to the south, clouds, rain, and snow are rare in winter. Nomads had to wait until the spring "monsoon" period for the often scant but precious rainfall. Nature, always surprising, could deliver spring and summer snow storms, hail and freezing rains, not infrequently bringing disaster for young animals.

In his book, *Fields on the Hoof*, Robert Ekvall described some of the emergencies the nomads faced and had to resolve in the course of their daily lives:

> "A grass fire threatens to burn the winter-quarters pasturage, or, out of control, does destroy it; traders try to drive infected livestock...through communal territory; scabies is discovered in the sheep herd; the horse herd is stampeded by a thunderstorm and takes off at high speed; wolves are sighted or suspicious tracks of unknown horsemen are seen; straying stock get caught in the bog or quicksand; oxen spill tenthold belongings along the trail and scatter with the pack ropes dragging; a rider's own mount gets dangerously trapped in deep snow or treacherous bog; the horse herd is driven off by raiders;...yak and mDZa cows sneak away to return to where they dropped last year's calves; the trail of the grain caravan is blocked by sudden spread of glare ice from spring seepage; rivers too deep to ford must be crossed in search of lost cattle."[3]

Though they lived an isolated lifestyle, many nomads traveled in winter to Lhasa and other market towns to barter with local farmers and householders. Nomads would trade many animal-produced products, such as butter and hides, in exchange for barley, tea, imported cloth, and other essentials of life. "The nomads from the northern parts of Tibet would come down to the farmlands to trade," we were told by Lama Kunga Rimpoche, who grew up on an estate in a village near Shigatse, some three hundred miles southwest of Lhasa, across the Brahmaputra River. "We allowed them to camp out on our fields. They set up tents. Each nomad owned thousands of sheep and yaks. We would let them stay for two or three weeks; and by the time they left all of our farmland was fertilized by the sheep and yaks."

Yak dung was essential to the life of nomads and all Tibetans. Applied generously to the ground, it enriched the soil and hastened the growing cycle for food production. This abundant and dependable output from the grazing yak also provided Tibetans with ample fuel for cooking and heat. As a fuel, dung was highly efficient and had few negative effects as it burned inside a tent. The dung was collected and carefully stored. Semi-nomads and farmers stored it on their rooftops. When large enough quantities were dried, it made an excellent substitute for bricks for building wall enclosures to protect tents from the harsh Tibetan winter.

Tibetans developed a niche in the natural hierarchy, along with other living beings in their environment, which honored the balance of nature and allowed for a sustained existence. And the elders, who passed the knowledge on from generation to generation of how to live with the land, remained within the family unit until the end of their years, making their inherited and acquired wisdom and experience always available to the young.

Hanga, a fifty-nine-year-old nomad woman from western Tibet, grew up near the shadows of sacred Mt. Kailas. In describing her early life, she told us: "I know that parents are very important and very dear. And I know the animals are equally important because we get our food and clothing from [them]. We even have a prayer about it that runs like this: 'May I be able to repay my parents' gratitude. May I be able to repay for the meat I have taken from the animals. May I be able to repay for the milk that I have drunk from the animals.' " When we asked her who taught her this prayer she said, "It is the elder people who taught us.... I don't think that the religion described much of such things."

It would be wrong to convey the idea that life was idyllic for the nomadic Tibetans, or that they uniformly were praiseworthy in carrying out their religious beliefs and being good neighbors. Some nomads were known to raid neighboring encampments to enrich their stock and to increase their share of wealth. This practice was a continued source of inter-tribal rivalry and retribution. It was said, however, that the thieves observed a code of honor. The bandits who did the raiding would not leave their victims without enough resources to survive where life was lived close to the margins.[4]

Admittedly, the nomadic lifestyle involved extreme hardship; however, the nomads' ability to bear these difficulties was remarkable, and in fact many nomads regarded themselves as an elite among those who lived on the soil, seeing a settled existence as undesirable.

NOTES

1. Walter Goldschmidt, "Theory and Strategy in the Study of Cultural Adaptability," American Anthropologist (1964), 405.
2. Melvyn C. Goldstein, and Cynthia M. Beall, *Nomads of Western Tibet: The Survival of a Way of Life* (Berkeley: University of California Press, 1990), 99.
3. Robert K. Ekvall, *Fields on the Hoof* (London: Holt, Rinehart & Winston, 1968), 87-88.
4. Norbu J. Thubten, and Colin M. Turnbill, *Tibet* (New York: Simon & Schuster, 1969), 40.

CHAPTER FOUR

The Reapers

"Eighteen great valleys of the south [Kham] are our birthplaces: ours, your sons' and grandsons'. When in summer we got to the pastureland [Amdo] we find there good grass. When in Autumn we go to our country, we find there good land."[1]

While separated perhaps by only a few thousand feet, nomads and the people who tilled the soil lived in different worlds. The nomad on his infrequent way to market with surplus wool, butter, or meat, might have shouted out to the farmers, "Salutations! people of the earthen house." In return he might be answered, "Greetings! man of the black tent," for this was how they frequently referred to one another, in dialects that were familiar yet different.

The valleys—some deep, narrow, and descending, and others wide and level—provided a more forgiving landscape than the high, windy plateaus. The majesty of the mountain vistas was still visible, but appeared farther away. For the farmers, pleasures and hardships varied notably from those of the nomads. Their diets and living conditions were created mainly from resources freely available in their milieu, but were connected with the high pastures that supplied them with resources derived from the yak, sheep, and goat. (See photo, p. 78)

In the higher valleys such as the Tsangpo and those in Amdo to the northeast, sudden hail storms and flooding, or excessive dry periods, often inflicted hardships. Similarly, on the threshold of the vegetative belt, where only grains and a few types of vegetables could be harvested, life was quite harsh. Being able to grow only one crop of grain per year made it important to husband surplus grain with special care for the inevitable lean years. Yak dung, the only source of fuel, was equally precious.

The Tsamgpo valley is the area in Tibet where the most intense cultivation takes place. Because of high mountains to the north and south, it is more protected from the weather than many of the higher regions of the country. Between seven and fourteen miles wide, with good drainage along the Yarlung Tsamgpo River and summer temperatures that rise to 80 degrees Fahrenheit, it is the most productive place to farm. In addition to a variety of grains, apples can be grown there. In the summer, the vast fields of blossoming mustard (used for making cooking oil) create a spectacular scene. Because of the weather, quality of the soil, and good drainage, it has the largest population of farmers in the country (See photo, p. 74).

The farmers depended not upon a great variety of resources, but wise management of what was available to them. We talked to Gendum, a sturdy farmer from Kham, who proudly said, "I am a very good plowman and all the people in my village compliment my work and I know the best way to plow the fields." Gendum had lived in one of the valleys not too far below the grazing ranges. "We grow barley, wheat, white barley, small peas, and we grow yungma [turnip]," he told us. "We have very huge turnips...Women cut the turnips into small pieces with a sickle and we dry it and in the winter we feed them to our domestic animals." Except for turnips, he said, "it is not our habit to grow and eat vegetables. What we eat is *tsampa*, flour, meat, milk, curd, and this is rich food. We also grow mustard on many fields. When you crush these mustards into a powder and then boil [it] in a huge iron pot, then the oil of a very pure and good quality comes out. Since we don't grow vegetables, we don't use this oil for cooking. We make offerings of butter lamp with this oil."

To bolster the needed resources, farmers living at this height would often hire themselves out to the nomad families to help with the shearing of the animals, or do the slaughtering and the skinning of the livestock. The nomads did not like to do this type of work. In a nomads' encampment the farmer helpers were fed cheese, butter, and meat, and paid for their labor in these and other goods only sparsely available down below.

Traditionally, barley was the main crop and the principal item in the diet of both nomads and farmers. Ground barley powder was the main commodity used in trade between them. Roasted and ground to a powder called *tsampa*, barley formed the basic diet of many Tibetans. Prepared in either uncooked form—as a paste—or baked as a bread, it had much of the nutritional values needed to sustain life. Monks in remote monasteries were known to live almost totally on *tsampa* along with the traditional tea with yak butter. This combination of nutrients has been found to be well suited to those living in high altitudes. For those who lived below seven thousand feet, with ample topsoil, there was a greater variety and abundance of food products of which nomads could only dream.

A farmer from a lower elevation boasted about the fact that in his area there were three types of barley for making *tsampa*—yellow, black, and a small variety—as well as five types of wheat of different sizes and colors. He reported that a variety of vegetables and fruits also grew in this region, but no mention was made of meat and dairy products being easily available.

The genetic diversity of edible grains has been an important feature of Tibetan ecology. Cultivation of a single grain type as a source of food would have interfered with the continuous development of several varieties of native wild species that evolved in this region. Since the occupation, however, the Chinese have placed emphasis on the use of just one strain of grain. Over time, this practice will weaken the genetic diversity of the species, and may put at risk people depending on a single strain that could be eradicated by a draught, pest infestation, or disease.

Just as the nomads created community through their ring of tents, the farmers maintained their dwellings close to one another, in a gathering of ten to fifteen houses—smaller than a village, but usually a sufficient number to provide a sense of place. The conscious sense of community that developed among farmers bound them together; through this informal organization they shared resources, exchanged family tasks, and provided mutual help. Because of the threat of thievery and banditry, not unknown in Tibet, communal life also provided greater security. Nomad encampments were much more vulnerable to banditry (See photo, p. 76).

The houses themselves, depending upon the availability of adobe and wood, were square structures, sometimes two stories. Large or small, they were solidly built. The designs used a minimum amount of wood, which was almost always gathered from nearby forests for the roof's beam structure. Wealth, of course, played a major role in the size and design of the house, with some families able to afford large structures having a great number of rooms, including a room used only as a shrine, and a room to store grains and other dried foods. Not infrequently, one saw neatly piled stacks of wood in front of the houses. Although used in times of emergency, this display of logs served more as a symbol of prestige.[2] (See photo, p. 98)

Like the nomad's tent, a Tibetan house was built solidly to achieve warmth in the worst of weather. The windows were usually made quite small to keep out the continuous wind and keep in the warmth. The main room was always the kitchen, where the family gathered around a continuously heated hearth to be with one another and drink quantities of butter tea. This nutritious drink provides ample calories to store up body fat for the coldest of times. It was the first thing a guest was offered coming into the house. The finely crafted Tibetan tea cup rarely had a chance to become emptied. On making tea, a *Khampa* (a person from Kham) gives this advice:

> *One, the best tea from China,*
> *Two, the pure dri butter of Tibet,*
> *Three, the white salt from the northern plains,*
> *All three from different places,*
> *All meeting in the copper pot,*
> *Yet how the tea is brewed*
> *is up to you, O tea maker.*[3]

Wealth aside, a Tibetan farming community was close knit. The Tibetans referred to the wealthier families as "big," and the others as "small." One former farmer named Gendum described the community's relationships: "Both the big and small families cultivate the fields at the same time," he told us. "If you haven't finished, then you can call even the wealthy people who finished cultivating their fields to help you." Gendum said that the wealthy families often had a number of hired workers. "People come to help us cultivate our fields," he continued, "but we don't have to pay, we don't have the system of paying money when somebody comes to help you. But they give wine and chang to those who come to help them. If a family builds a house, it takes many days and the villagers go and help them for many days, transporting stone to build the house."

Compared to the nomads, farmers living in or near villages marked their lives by a more intense relationship to the monasteries and, as a result, engaged in a broader range of Buddhist practices. Monasteries were almost always closer to the agricultural valleys than to the high plateaus. As a consequence, farm families were frequently able to visit monasteries during the many festivals and holidays requiring participation in religious rites. (A three-day walk might be considered close.) Monks frequently were hired to visit the homes to provide *pujas*, or ceremonies, to mark the coming and going of life, protect family members from illnesses, and propitiate the elements to provide good weather and prosperous times. During these visits the families shared their abode with the monks. It was a time when children developed an understanding of the need to respect the land and the prohibition against harming other life.

This closer association with the *dharma* (the essence of Buddhist teachings) tended to make the farming families more sensitive and responsive to the do's and don'ts of their faith. Farmers faced a complex spiritual issue: in order to survive, they needed to know when to plow the land, but Buddhist teaching admonished people not to disturb the earth, which was sacred (mining was also forbidden). As a result of the constraint against digging the soil, farmers often felt they were creating negative karma. What was one to do when this was their only livelihood? They compensated in their daily living by special acts of goodness or by making offerings in the temples. It was not uncommon for the nomads to jokingly scorn farmers for the ungodly practice of tilling the soil, which they themselves had no need to do.

As we have seen, Buddhist beliefs extended to the protection of the forests and the disapproval of cutting trees. Monasteries often had sacred forests within their domain. Chimi, a retired farmer from Juba Drong, in Kham, lived near the border region in

Yunan Province. He was quite articulate and could read and write Tibetan, and speak English. Chimi told us about the control of tree cutting in his native village. "If sacred trees are cut," he said, for three months the farmer who cut them "has to offer donations to the various monasteries in the region.... The person then has to plant nine more trees for cutting one. The person also has to pay for the cost of the tree and the money has to be donated into the public funds to be used for religious purposes. The wood he cut will not be given to him. It will be taken for public consumption. If any outsider cuts a tree, then severe punishment would be given. His hands or legs would be damaged, but no life sentence or death sentence would be passed."

Without the use of machine-powered tools—without even the wheel—the life of the farmer, male and female, was experienced as burdensome, requiring its own type of discipline. The *dzo*, a yak-cattle hybrid, pulling a hand-crafted plow, provided the "backbone" of farm work. In poorer families without yaks the wife often served as a substitute.

Every effort was made to get the planting started as the annual growth cycle began. To insure correct timing, it was customary to get an authoritative opinion. Jamyang, a young immigrant from Kham, stated, "We generally consult an astrologer so that we can begin on an auspicious day." He described the rituals used to prepare for planting: "That day my mother would dress me up in the best clothes, we would burn incense and would take the incense around the fields and offer our prayers. The *dzo's* horns and neck are decorated and the fields are plowed. We would also eat very good food that day. Our prayers are: that we may have good crops, then all sentient beings have enough to eat—all kinds of beings, whether human beings, insects, animals, everyone."

Many Tibetan farmers reported that the fields were usually kept fallow for at least a year. One farmer from Kham told us: "People keep the land fallow, especially those fields which are on slopes where continuous cultivation has taken all of the fertility. These lands are kept fallow for a period of up to four years." Keenly aware of the need for nutrients in the soil, Tibetans relied heavily on animal dung, seeing it as a sort of magic potion—freely given by nature—that supports life. In earlier years, artificial fertilizers were never known (See photo, p. 99).

The Tibetan New Year (Losar) begins in March, at the time of the first moon. In some areas, the celebration of the new year included a ritual performed by the younger men, a dangerous combination of acrobatics and horseback riding. As in similar rituals in other Central Asian societies, the horsemen leaned down while galloping full speed to pick up an object off the ground. Teams competed with one another, showing off their agility in the contest. Other games required shooting arrows at stationary targets while riding by them at full speed (See photo, p. 65).

During this period, the land was prepared for planting. Copious amounts of dung were spread on the fields, to be trampled on first by the youths on their wild horseback rides, and then by the *dzo* with their heavy hooves. The rocks were cleared from the field, which was then completely fenced off with whatever materials were available, to protect it from the wild animals in the area and the trampling of passers-by.

The preparation of the fields was not a very appealing task, especially for the women. One woman from Amdo reported:

> The difficult work that the farmer has is just before planting their crop in the spring. They have to clean all their fields, and take dzo dung and sheep dung and transport it to the fields as fertilizers...they have to remove the stones and they have to burn the grasses and other dry plants. This is very difficult work for the farmers. This work is mainly done by the womenfolk and when they come home in the evening, all over their body, from head to feet they are covered in dust and they look just like millers.
>
> Some families transport *dzo* and sheep dung on the yak's back. Those who don't have yaks, have to transport the fertilizers on their backs. The womenfolk carry the dry dung to their [closer] fields on their backs and the menfolk take the fertilizer or the dried cow and sheep dung on horseback to the far fields.

Chimi, who is from Amdo, described the planting and the involvement of the community in this vital activity:

> Helping hands of neighbors will be called on. Labor is exchanged in such work.

> Sometimes the people get the branches of trees, crush them into pieces and prepare them for making the manure. The process would take the whole day. By the second moon, the fields are ready for planting. Sowing begins with the father of the family putting the seeds in, or the elder of the family, so it is sown evenly by experienced hands.
>
> Sowing is a period of hectic activities—not all hard work. Chang [Tibetan beer] and food has to be ready from the very beginning, because during the sowing season a lot of helping hands are required—some for sowing the seeds, some for covering them up, some for plowing, some for leveling...some for removing the weeds and grass. Those who have plows and manual resources help the poor families in this work. The spirit of helping each other is very strong. No money is charged for the helping.... At this time the families perform religious services at home...and go on pilgrimages.

In addition to the heavy work in the fields, Chimi told us: "The women have to do most of the household work, in terms of cooking and everything. So that women have much more work than the husbands. The men do not do the household work, but they take the responsibility of the entire family—how to look after the members of the family. They shoulder the main responsibility of the family, but they don't do the household work."

Throughout Tibet, but especially in the higher valleys in U-Tsang and in Amdo, there was always the threat of losing crops due to bad weather. In the West, when the weather report is aired nightly on the radio and television, it is hard to understand how people would cope where there is little accurate information or even help, following disaster. Traditionally, farmers continued to use animistic methods of guarding against the tragic consequences of the destructive forces of weather. Gendum, a farmer from Kham, told us:

> When there was a hailstorm, we requested *ngapas* [local shamans] to protect our fields; keep them from being destroyed. These weather men, they would put daggers all over our fields and these daggers are blessed by them. So whenever there is a hail storm or thunderstorm, the weathermen recite some mantras and they meditate, and in this

> way some powerful *ngagpas* can protect the fields from being destroyed by hailstorms. Through the power of the *ngagpas* they lead the hailstorms to the rocky mountains and other mountains where there were no fields, so they really can protect the fields. We invited *ngapas* when the crops grew about a foot high and we asked them to protect the crops until the harvest. We left the *ngapas* in a small house over the mountains and whenever there came a hailstorm, thunderstorm, the *ngagpas* put on a black hat and they held big swords in their hands and they did some gestures with their hand and thus they could stop the hailstorm. But there are some powerless *ngapas*...who cannot stop the hailstorms, which eventually destroy the crops.

Like the seed-planting phase, the time of harvest included celebrations, both religious and festive. In farming communities, the harvest was a communal affair; help was provided by neighboring farmers who knew they would be repaid in kind. Following consultation with the local weather specialist and almanacs if they had them, the village headmen designated the day to begin the reaping. The gathering of all available farm folk made it possible to harvest the entire crop quickly, before bad weather set in and spoiled the harvest. Although it was crucial to save the harvest, time was allowed for ritual festive eating and drinking chang, a mandatory part of the proceedings.

The festivals following the harvests had special meaning to the Tibetan farm families and signaled a time for the community to come together and reaffirm long-held social ties. Due to Tibet's unique topography, members of the community who lived far apart could meet and celebrate their hard work during these times. These celebrations provided continuity of the culture and a chance for new male-female bonds to begin (See photos, pp. 97, 100, 101).

In his informative book about Aten, the Khampa warrior, Jamyang Norbu described the celebrations: "Friends and relatives from other villages came to help. Great pots of ale were brought out to the fields and there was much singing and feasting as the sheaves of golden barley were cut and stacked. Gargantuan meals were served to all, and even after the work was done, the young men and women would tirelessly dance, sing, and romance around the big bonfires in the night."[4] The chanting began as the sheaves came down, evoking the spiritual dimension as well as communal enthusiasm: "Now prepare altogether, / Now yourself exert some force, / Say Mani and get ready, / Now Mani Padme prepare, / Now say Mani Padme Hung Re."[5] The chant was repeated with additional verses singing out Buddhist praises.

Chimi comes from a warmer part of Amdo where it is possible to grow two crops per year. "After one crop is harvested, then the growing of another crop starts," she told us. "We have a bow-and-arrow shooting ceremony where the people run in the fields. You see about two hundred or three hundred people running in the fields. Strangely, these crops, instead of being destroyed, will give a better harvest. Again you see the *dzo*. When it enters a field and eats the crop, there is no fine for the owners and no punishments. The people will just drive the animal away calmly and politely. The people believe that this animal has a right to eat the crops because it has put so much labor into plowing and cultivating the fields."

Following the harvest the thrashing began. A practice was to lay the sheaths of grain in a flat, dry place, and lead the *dri*, or a horse, dragging a huge stone around in a circle over the grain until it began to separate from the chaff. Thrashing was followed by winnowing, in which the barley became separated from the remainder of the seed's outer covering. Here, weather was also a serious determinant. The winds could blow favorably, assisting in the separation process or threatening to blow away the product of the year's toil in short order. Most winnowing was done outside.

Some fortunate families had houses with internal courtyards where this final phase of the harvest was carried out. The usual custom was to store the year's supply of barley in hardy bags woven out of yak hair. For those who obtain their grain from supermarkets, it is hard to realize the amount and varied work required to grow, process, and bring to market a mere handful of grain! Like other native peoples, the Tibetans understood this well and carefully divided the year's harvest, setting aside part for the next year's food supply, part for next year's planting, an ample amount to save for harder times, the amount of grain needed to pay taxes, and an amount to serve for offerings to the monks or to lay upon the monasteries' altars.

Soon after they were able to walk, children were active participants in each phase of farm life. Responsibilities would soon be assigned to them, but the Tibetans tended to be lenient and allowed ample opportunity for frolicsome play. Without manufactured toys, simple objects such as a ball of wool, a stone, or a shapely piece of wood, or beads and ribbons for the girls, could be enough to get a game started (See photo, p. 79). The farm animals were great objects of affection and play. Being on the scene for the birth of a young lamb or kid provided great joy. Not infrequently, the young animal would be adopted as a special playmate.

Although animal husbandry was not the principal source of work and income for the farmers, they raised sheep and goats. Keeping these animals was a sign of affluence. The "big families" often had sheep and goats numbering into the hundreds, while poorer families only possessed a few. Having farm animals represented a form of security against a poor harvest, as they could always be traded for barley, or *tsampa*, if necessary.

People from the farming villages were in an advantageous position to engage in trade. Living between the market towns and nomadic areas, they shuttled wool and other animal products from the mountain pastures to Lhasa and outlying towns. While there, they would purchase goods to sell to the nomads—blocks of pressed tea and the few manufactured items thought of as necessities.

Throughout Tibet, on the sloping mountainsides, in forests, and on the lower mountain tops, grow a vast variety of medicinal herbs that make up both the Tibetan and Chinese pharmacopoeia. Many of the herbs were so much in demand that they fetched excellent prices. Farm people of all ages are easily able to identify these herbs, most of which grow close to the ground. In regions where these plants and bushes abound, Tibetans will be found harvesting the herbs to take to the market place.

These medicinal herbs have been exported to China for untold years. A number of interviewees described an herb called yasegumbo that is highly valued in China and is an important source of income for farm families. Tibetans from different areas have developed a special eye for locating it. Its strange appearance and life cycle is described by one Tibetan as follows: "In the summer it is a grass and in the wintertime it turns into a worm, and goes underground. The grass is found in abundance when the snow has melted, somewhere in the fourth month…the mountains remain filled with this grass. At first you see a wiggly worm coming up, then it turns to a grass. By the sixth month the plant has no value. Some people will collect in a day about three-thousand [segments] of this grass."[6]

As we have seen, the life styles of nomads and farmers were identifiably different. While it might seem that each way of life has equivalent hardships and compensations, Tibetans themselves believe otherwise. In our interviews, both groups agreed that the nomads, in spite of the altitude and horrendous weather, lived superior lives. It might seem that the frequent taking down of the tents, the changing of campsites, and resettling in another area would make this existence burdensome. The daily milking of scores of female yaks by the women and the need for the men to be conscious of the safety of the animals around the clock also take their toll. However, the nomads repeatedly stated that their lives were easy since nature provided everything they needed. The farmers did not disagree.

The nomads' excellent survival within their environment is, in large part, due to the fact that with just a few key resources, they live in a sustainable way. They depend on farmers only for barley. Farmers, on the other hand, are quite dependent upon resources that originate in the high grasslands. Meat, butter, cheese, the wool and leather for their garments, and other products are all obtained from the nomads. Furthermore, the income from their agricultural work is insufficient. Farmers need to engage in active trade, and do seasonal work for the nomads, to make ends meet.

Robert Ekvall, an anthropologist who spent years living among the nomads, compared the physical conditions of nomads and farmers:

> The superiority of the nomad in physique and health is also marked. Such was the opinion of Dr. Rees, who traveled with us for about three months, visiting both nomadic and sedentary communities. We examined over three thousand men and women and had ample opportunity to form an opinion. In spite of the great exposure and hardship incident to nomadic life, the nomads were far healthier than the sedentary people. There was much higher incidence of syphilis among the sedentary people than among

> the nomads, although there seemed to be more gonorrhea among the latter. Dr. Rees found no leprosy among the nomads but a high incidence among the farming people.[7]

The differences appear to be explained by their different diets. Although the nomads and farmers ate the same types of food (except that vegetables were unavailable to the nomads), they consumed different quantities of each type. It appears that the farmers had a much harder time obtaining sufficient high-protein and high-fat foods, which are important to maintaining health in Tibet's harsh climate.

Differences in the quality of life also reflected differences in the actual monetary wealth of the average nomad and average farmer. The farmers owned houses and obviously had other physical possessions (those that a nomad could not carry along with his collapsible portable home), but the combined value of the farmer's house possessions and livestock compared unfavorably with the average wealth of the nomad. The value of the nomads' closely woven yak-hair tents was considerable. These, along with the market value of their yaks, sheep, and goats, amounted to more than the value of what the farmers owned. It was the nomads' practice to always try to increase the size of their livestock herds. This was their insurance. Understanding these factors makes it clear why farmers, if they could, would obtain livestock and become what are called semi-nomads, setting up nomadic camps where grasses were plentiful enough for grazing livestock.

Previous to the communist domination of Tibet, the land was usually owned by large estate owners or monasteries, both big and small. As in feudal times in Europe, the land was parceled out through a system of reciprocity between the landowners and the nomads and farmers.

Payments to the owners were made in products of the land, the amount given was determined by the size of the land allotment. The nomads were expected to pay the land owners or monasteries by providing wool, meats, skins, and dairy products. The farm families provided such items as oils, meats, dairy products, and some handcrafted items. In addition to providing consumable supplies, in some cases the farmers were expected to provide a certain number of free labor days. In most cases, the

In the spring, young riders, while galloping at full speed, compete to retrieve a scarf off the ground (Kham).

Nomads' tents, made from tightly woven yak hair, provide insulation against rain and wind. The black cloth cover allows heat to be stored inside during the heat of the day (Amdo).

A community of tents belonging to an extended family, or clan, that shares the available grazing areas.

A yak caravan unloading freshly shorn wool.

In central Tibet, abundant thermal activity provides hot springs in areas still accessible to Tibetan nomads.

Inside a nomad family's tent, a traditional meal of yogurt, yak-butter tea, and stew is prepared.

Both young and older Tibetan women wear their hair in braids. This young girl smiles as her mother braids locks of her hair (Amdo).

Nomads traditionally herd yaks and other livestock with the help of a slingshot which makes a loud crack as a stone is catapulted.

Tibetan children learn valuable skills by watching their elders in action. Here, a child gets first-hand experience in herding while on horseback.

Well-tended fields in central Tibet, shortly after spring crops have been sown (U-Tsang). It is no longer common for Tibetans to own or use prime farming land.

Some farmers were fortunate enough to have an irrigation ditch and regular water supply during the warmer months.

A small farming village in U-Tsang.

Preparing to visit family members, these Tibetans start their journey in yak-skin boats called coracles. Few Tibetans today own such boats or can afford extended journeys (U-Tsang).

A small farming village in Kham. A number of Tibetan exiles we spoke with in Dharamsala told us about being forced off their land by Chinese authorities or settlers. With the massive resettling of Chinese in Tibet, and the many deaths of Tibetans from starvation and violence, Tibetans are now a minority in their own country.

A young girl takes time to play with a hoop. Tibetan children rarely have toys to play with but find ways to spend their free time.

Daily religious observances have been vital to the Tibetan way of life for centuries. The woman shown here is kindling incense for an offering during planting season

rights to the land passed on from family to family. Often, one of the nomads or farmers would keep track of the allotments and the payments made by each family.

A number of the refugees described themselves as semi-nomads, or *samarogs*, whose families held tenure on the land for traditional farming. These families were often larger than the average nomadic group. Typically, they had accumulated enough resources in terms of livestock to be able to maintain land for growing grain. They also had family members to bring their livestock—yak, sheep, or goats—into the higher elevations where the grasses grow thick.

In essence, the family was split between the high pastures and the lower farming areas. During the times when more help was needed for the planting and harvesting, some of the family members descended to help with these important functions. One young man from a semi-nomadic family said that it was his particular job to run up and down the mountainside replenishing the nomads with *tsampa* and returning with fresh butter and yogurt for his family.

Some *samarog* groups bring their animals back to the village each evening, herding them by shooting stones flung from a yak-wool slingshot. In other *samarog* communities, the men take the herds to summer pasture high in the mountains, returning to their villages in late autumn. According to Robert Ekvall, families that became semi-nomads were moving up the economic ladder by expanding their economic potential to include the greatest resources available.

Not all Tibetans were as dependent on the natural environment as nomads and farmers. Traders held a unique niche in society, serving as economic and intellectual bridges between sequestered Tibet and the outside world. Besides increasing the flow of wool to India and salt to Nepal, they imported a number of products that supplemented the relatively nonmaterialistic Tibetan lifestyle. Chief among these was black tea, an essential part of the Tibetan diet (some monks and nomads, especially in the colder, drier regions, drank up to forty cups a day). Traders also brought back ingredients such as Chinese ginseng and Indian spices, used in Tibetan medicines, as well as luxury items like porcelain, gold, silk brocade, and silver. Among Tibet's more exotic exports, ethnographer Peter Gold cites white yak tails: an unlikely item which made its way to the United States, where it was used to make Santa Claus beards.[8]

Another social class, mostly visible in the few urban centers, was the Tibetan aristocracy. Drawn from royal blood lines or from more humble families with extraordinary religious standing, such as the parents of an incarnate lama, these nobles governed the secular affairs of the Tibetan people. But even though they were the wealthiest class, the nobility were not the highest ranking. It was Tibet's monastic community, or *sangha*, that held the greatest sway over people's lives, especially in the ethical and spiritual realms. Virtually all urban centers, however small, had their own monasteries and nunneries. Every family desired to see at least one child enter the monastery as a young monk, and to complete the arduous ten- to fifteen-year education leading to becoming a lama.

NOTES

1. Peter Gold, "Tibetans and Their Way of Life," *ChöYang (*Kuala Lampur, Malasia: Graphic Press, 1991), 278.
2. Robert Ekvall, *The Sedentary and Nomadic Tibetans in Cultural Relations on the Kansu-Tibetan Border* (Chicago: University of Chicago Press, 1939), 72.
3. Jamyang Norbu, *Horseman in the Snow* (Dharamsala, India: Information Office, Central Tibetan Secretariat, 1979), 7.
4. Jamyang Norbu, *Horseman in the Snow,* 35.
5. Marion Duncan, *Love Songs and Proverbs of Tibet* (London: The Mitre Press, 1961), 15.
6. Several of the nomads we interviewed described this plant.
7. Ekvall, *The Sedentary and Nomadic Tibetans*, 82.
8. Gold, *Tibetans and Their Way of Life*, 281.

CHAPTER FIVE

Endangered Land

"The Tibetan government limited mining and exploitation of natural resources to avoid disrupting not only the animal life and ecological system, but the unseen creatures believed to dwell there. Moreover, it officially organized a great many rituals, which sought to please the local deities and ensure harmonious natural conditions."[1]

As we have seen, Tibet was for centuries distinguished by its isolation. That isolation and the harsh natural conditions of the country forced Tibetans to develop a way of life that protected their delicate homeland and its limited resources and, at the same time, provided sustenance for their survival. But that way of life and the protection it afforded the environment of Tibet changed drastically in the 1950s, when China invaded this virtually defenseless land and ultimately took total control.

Tibet became an independent political entity in 127 B.C., when the Yarlung Dynasty came into being. Tibet's formal relationship with China dates from the seventh century A.D. The Tibetan king, Songten Gampo, who endorsed Buddhism as Tibet's state religion, married Chinese Princess Wen Chegin in 823. The princess brought with her a magnificent statue of Buddha, which is still in the Jokhang Temple in Lhasa. This historic marriage was commemorated by a stone pillar which, at least until recently, stood in front of the Potala Palace. The inscription clearly delineated the boundaries of each nation and declared their individual sovereignty, stating that each should be happy within its own boundaries.

By the thirteenth century, the Mongol tribes expanded their vast empire eastward into the territory of China. In order to assure national security, Tibet's ruling power established an agreement with Kublai Khan, the Mongol leader, under which Tibet would remain politically loyal to the Mongol kings; in exchange, the Mongol nation would accept and honor the religious teachings of Tibetan Buddhism. When Kublai Khan finally conquered China, he chose a Sakya Lama from a leading Tibetan monastery as the religious leader of his vast empire.

The Mongol people are closely related to the Tibetans and have close religious and cultural ties. Even so, under the Mongol Empire, Tibet remained independent. Following the break-up of the Mongol domination of China during the long rule of the Ming Dynasty, from the fourteenth to the seventeenth centuries, Tibet had no formal relationship or ties to China. However, when the Manchus from Manchuria came to power and established the Qing Dynasty in 1644, the Dalai Lama agreed to act as spiritual guide for the Manchu emperor. In exchange, he accepted the emperor's protection from political pressures from the outside. This religious patronage-political protection partnership continued until the fall of the Manchus in 1911. The current Chinese government uses this historical relationship to claim that Tibet has always been part of China.

Over time, the Manchus frequently attempted to exert more control over Tibet. For instance, when Tibet was invaded from the south by the Gurkhas of Nepal, and when it was invaded from the west by the Mongolians, the Chinese sent troops in to protect Tibet and, at the same time, expanded Chinese power.

The Chinese also used the office of the Amban in Lhasa as a means of gaining influence in Tibet. The Amban was a kind of ambassador whose role was to keep an eye on Tibet's foreign affairs. At most, the presence of the Amban and the Chinese expeditionary forces in Tibet amounted to little more than a guarantor of Tibet's autonomy against outside powers. Throughout this period, there was never a time when Tibet was an integral part of, or administered by, China.

Early in this century the British invaded Tibet, coming up from India through Bhutan. Their purpose was to force Tibet to open up as a trading partner and to insure that the Russians did not get there before them. A peace agreement was signed between Britain and Tibet at the Lhasa Convention. China was having problems with the British and other Western countries, including Portugal and Germany, which established colonies along the Pacific coast. Wanting to maintain some control over Tibet, China sent forces to Lhasa in 1910 to insure its presence. However, by 1911, China was still in revolt and the long-standing Manchu Dynasty ended. Tibet took advantage of this change and succeeded in forcing the Chinese troops to surrender. The forces were sent back to China. Tibet remained an independent nation until the communists started their takeover in 1949.

When China invaded Tibet in 1949, the Chinese stated that their goal was to liberate Tibet from its feudal rule, and claimed that Tibet had always been part of China. It was clear that Tibetans did not invite or want the Chinese to take over their land, nor did they ever have the opportunity to express their opinions in a plebiscite on the occupation. The Chinese first moved into the province of Kham, to the east. Despite Chinese promises to help in modernization, Tibetans soon realized that the Chinese goal was to completely absorb Tibet into their communist revolution.

The inhabitants of Kham began an active resistance, with thousands of Khampa men and women joining the guerrilla movement. It was only gradually that the full force of the occupation was felt in central Tibet, where the country's capital and main population centers are located.

The Dalai Lama, who was fifteen years old at the time of the invasion, sought to soften the impact of the occupation and to keep as much as possible of the government in the hands of Tibetans. By 1959, the Dalai Lama realized that the Chinese had not been dealing honestly with him and his people. Understanding that his own personal freedom was in jeopardy and that he could do the most for his people if he were outside Tibet, he escaped to India to continue the struggle from exile.

Though China refused to admit it at the time of the invasion, there were many reasons the Chinese wanted to control the "Roof of the World." First of all, Tibet, which borders on India and the former Soviet Union, could provide a strategic buffer for China. And as has been noted, China coveted Tibet's untapped natural resources—forests, minerals, hydropower, agricultural products, and livestock. In fact, the Chinese name for Tibet, *Xizang*, which means "Western Treasure House," tells much about how China viewed Tibet.

The Cultural Revolution brought devastation throughout both China and Tibet. The Red Guards succeeded in destroying the practices and cultural institutions that were the most precious to the people in Tibet. Nothing was more precious to the population than the monasteries. The monasteries were like universities for the education of monks and nuns; they were places where Tibetans went to pay homage to their deities and restore their sense of well-being. Monasteries were also museums of Buddhist art with ancient sacred objects of great pride and value.

Starting in 1967, within a period of three years, 6,254 monasteries were systematically destroyed and emptied of their precious artwork, which was sent to Beijing. They were bombed until nothing was left but the bare walls. Tibetans themselves were forced to participate in the dismantling of the contents of the monasteries. Objects not sent to China for storage were either desecrated in the market places or burnt in bonfires. Although these heinous acts were done under the leadership of the Red Guards, the devastation of the monasteries was the outcome of anti-religious policies established by the Chinese before the Cultural Revolution (See photos, pp. 102–105).

Although the monasteries as such were not a part of the natural surroundings, they were almost always situated in the most auspicious locations, surrounded by forests that were held sacred. These structures, which blended in with nature, were "zones of peace," where wildlife was allowed to roam undisturbed, and living centers where the lessons on compassion for all living things were taught. Monasteries represented the ecclesiastical link between the people and their environment. Today, approximately 10 percent of them have been rebuilt by the Tibetans. In 1997, their use was severely restricted by the Chinese, both in the number that were allowed to stay open and in the number of monks allowed to reside in them.

Namgyal, a former nomad from the Chanthang region, left Tibet when he was fifteen years old. He told us that today, when Tibetans want to rebuild monasteries, "we have to buy our wood from them [the Chinese]. Rebuilding of the monasteries all over Tibet, including my area, is slowly done by and from money contributed by the Tibetans. Not a single penny ever came from the Chinese treasury, or the government or the communist party. Yet when some visitors would come, we have been strictly advised to inform the visitors that the monasteries have been rebuilt by the gracious donation from the Chinese government. This is not true."

In monasteries throughout Tibet, the Chinese became increasingly sensitive to any sign of protest by the nuns and monks. In the spring of 1997, the Chinese government began a "Cultural-Revolution-style re-education" program in the monasteries. Tibetans in Lhasa described the sessions as witch hunts, designed to instill fear and obedience amongst the monks, and cull out those monks who are not willing to go along with Chinese policies on [the teaching of] Tibetan History and the role of Buddhism in Tibetan society.[2]

As the occupation has continued, the Chinese attitude toward the environment—that man and society are above nature and that nature is to be disposed of at the will of society—has become increasingly evident. In light of this attitude, the Chinese view Tibetans, who have lived mainly by the laws of nature, as inadequate and ignorant. The Chinese believe Tibetans must be forced to change.

Tashi Gyaltsen, an exiled abbot of Dip Tse-Chok-Ling Monastery now living in Dharamsala, described the changes that have been imposed. "Prior to the 1950s," he told us, "we did not pay much attention to worldly things, we were mainly interested in the religious aspects of life. Then the Chinese came and a lot of changes have taken place in Tibet, even to the extent that most of our forests have been cut down, grass, birds, minerals, and wild and domestic animals have been taken. The Chinese say this is for our well-being, but of course they have not done anything good for us—everything is bad for Tibet."

The Chinese system replaces natural processes with a reliance on technology to meet basic needs. Disregarding the balance of nature, it consumes nature's products to meet immediate needs and then ignores the long-range consequence of its acts. By singling out nature as an important consideration in the drive toward "progress," the Chinese have systematically depleted resources without accountability to the Tibetans whose land they occupy.

Under economic development methods introduced by the Chinese, a vast array of wildlife species have been depleted or endangered by, among other methods, organized hunts using machine guns to mow the animals down. As Dhondub Choedon, a Tibetan who worked on a commune for many years before escaping from Tibet in 1973, observed that even though their own "rules forbid killing...Chinese solders go on organized hunts, using automatic machine-guns. In some areas, there are special brigades who kill wild animals indiscriminately. They carry away the meat in lorries, and exported valuables like musk and fur to China."[3] Tashi Gyaltsen adds, "When we had our independence, there wasn't anyone who harmed or killed animals."

While on a 1943 expedition to study the Amnye Machin Mountains, Leonard Clark, an explorer and the author of *The Marching Wind*, described an area at the bend of the Yellow River as "one of the last unspoiled big game paradises remaining in Asia."[4] And Purba, who escaped to Dharamsala from Kham, said that before the Chinese arrived, if someone killed a deer, "he would be fined. He would have to say mantras and also he would have to raise new prayer flags."

The list of endangered species in Tibet is large—in 1990, the International Union for Conservation of Nature and Natural Resources listed eighteen species of wildlife and twelve species of birds in Tibet as endangered.[5] But as early as 1981, when he led an expedition of naturalists to the Amnye Machin region, Galen Rowell, a well-known wildlife photographer from California, could see that things were not right. The group's Chinese hosts had promised they would see a "wealth of rare birds and animals...thick virgin forests where deer, leopards, and bear thrived, a snow line alive with hordes of gazelles, wild asses and rare musk deer." Rowell continued, "For three weeks, we walked over a hundred miles in all. We saw virtually nothing. The wildlife had disappeared."[6]

And when Purba went back to his home to visit his father after his prison term ended, he said, "There had always been a white bird, the 'Jako' in my region. Its head was red, feet red, the body white, tail black—it was very big and its meat was known to be very delicious. In my country, nobody killed it. At the monastery, the monks would give it food and many hundreds of these birds could be seen at the monastery. Now, I have not seen any of these birds."

Chinese authorities are cooperating—up to a point—with naturalists from abroad who are searching for ways to protect specific wildlife species. Today, China has its own endangered species law that restricts hunting. The law covers the Tibetan antelope, snow leopard, giant panda, wild yak, Asian wild ass, Tibetan red panda, musk deer, and muli pika, all indigenous to the Tibetan Plateau. Unfortunately, a principal threat to all of these species is the continuing loss of habitat caused by deforestation. Adding to the problem is the lack of education for those living on the plateau about the need for conservation.

But the major factor contributing to the continued slaughter of endangered species is inadequate enforcement. There are not enough game wardens to do the policing—a scarcity that results from a lack of commitment on the part of the Chinese authorities to saving endangered species. In fact, the Chinese continue to organize hunting expeditions for wealthy Americans and Europeans who pay up to $35,000 to bag one animal of the same endangered species the government claims to protect.[7]

In recent years, the Chinese have established wildlife reserves as protected areas. These include the Chomolungma Nature Reserve in the shadow of Mount Everest, the Qinghai Nature Reserve in Amdo and, most recently, the Changthang Reserve in the vast northwestern reaches of the plateau. While these reserves are intended to protect wildlife, they remain understaffed, and rich rewards for pelts, bones, musk, and trophy heads make it commonplace to find body parts of protected species on the open market in China's larger cities as well as in Lhasa (See photo, p. 109). The Dalai Lama's personal physician, Dr. Tenzin Choedrak, told us bear paws, for example, which the Chinese believe have significant medicinal value, fetch handsome prices.

Between 1959 and 1985, under Chinese rule, clear-cutting of forests harvested more than an estimated $54 billion worth of wood.[8] "In 1949," according to the Tibetan Government-In-Exile, "Tibet's ancient forests covered 221,800 square kilometers. By 1985, they stood at 134,000 square kilometers."[9] Robbie Barnett, an Englishman who heads the Tibet Information Network in London, states that the Chinese continue to cut trees and transport the lumber back to China. "Fifty fully-laden timber trucks an hour" passed Barnett making their way toward China from Tibet.[10] (See photos, pp. 110, 111)

In 1995, two observers took a census of lumber trucks traveling from Tibet east to Chengdu, in China. One observer's "count of truck loads encountered between Chengdu and Kanding totaled 467 during ten hours on the road." They were large trees sawed off to fit the length of the truck. The other observer traveling between Luding and Chengdu "counted 380 logging trucks" in a period of a day. The average truck carried twenty-five logs, but in one instance "one giant log filled the entire truck. It would have taken three people to encircle its circumference."[11] Judging from the size of the trees described, they most likely come from virgin stands of trees located in Kham.

"In my region," said Purba, who originally came from Kham, "there are many thousands of people who cut down the trees. The trees were very good, really tall and big. The Chinese cut down all the trees.... Now if a Tibetan cuts a tree, he will be imprisoned. The Chinese also fine him."

Deforestation is responsible for another environmental problem: erosion. Talking about his return to Kham after his imprisonment, Purba said, "When I went again, there were hardly any forests, and there were many areas where the soil had been eroded and where no vegetation grew. Because of that, there is a lot of water running down this area and it's becoming heavily eroded. It was a sad sight to see."

And in 1980, Dr. Choedrak, the Dalai Lama's physician, returned to his favorite forest glen to collect some specific "precious herbs," following his seventeen-year imprisonment. As he reached the top of the hill where the herbs had grown in abundance, he found the area stark and barren, denuded of plant life. "The Chinese method of extracting timber from steep slopes," Dr. Choedrak observed, "is to dig a six-foot hole at the base of the trees and then explode dynamite to bring them down. The entire root system is then exposed and the top soil is scattered, thus increasing the effects of erosion."

When the Chinese first occupied Tibet, most of the forests were beyond reach. Since then, they have built a comprehensive road system to facilitate removal of lumber from the eastern and southern parts of the country. By clear-cutting timber on steep slopes and subsequently dragging it to the roads, the Chinese have loosened soil and created deep gullies, causing landslides and silting of rivers below. Even the vice-minister of forestry for the People's Republic of China, Dong Zhiyon, has criticized these methods of harvesting wood. "The wood-processing industry [in Tibet] is administered in the same way as mining. There is no regulation for regeneration, tending, and resource management"[12] (See photos, pp. 106–108).

It is not just erosion and rock falls that are causing river blockages; log jams and other debris are a problem as well. Traveling for two days along the Min River in southeastern Tibet, leading to the Yangtse, Robbie Barnett of the Tibet Information Network "saw nothing but log jams along the entire length."[13]

The environmental consequences of Tibet's deforestation can be felt in other Asian countries, not just Tibet. The result is that in India's Brahmaputra basin, annual floods, a feature of life in the area, are increasing dramatically. Some environmentalists believe the flooding in Bangladesh in recent years is due, at least in part, to the inability of denuded mountains upstream in Tibet to hold moisture from the monsoon rains.

In addition to Bangladesh, yearly flooding is a common occurrence in southern Nepal, through which the Ganges River flows. India has also had damage to its rice fields from flooding in the Ganges and Brahmaputra Rivers. In Myamar, Burma, the Irriwadi River is also subject to the land-use influences which originate in Tibet. More research must be done to quantify the total impact of China's timber removal practices.

Change in the quantity of Tibet's ground cover, such as through overgrazing and deforestation, is believed by climatologist Elmer Reiter to be affecting the weather of all of East Asia. The overgrazing of formerly green areas has led to desertification, and the disappearance of vast amounts of green forests increases the evaporation of moisture, affecting cloud cover. Dr. Reiter points out that the weather patterns in Tibet, affected by the amount of forest and grasslands that have been depleted, have a measurable effect on the weather patterns in adjacent regions of Southeast Asia and

China. He observed that this change already "could have produced noticeable effects in the form of decreased summer precipitation in India."[14]

Asked if the Chinese are doing anything about reforestation, Jamyang said, "Yes, they do it, but the young saplings do not grow very well because the land is not very good now. Only a few are growing.... In summer you need to water these saplings, because they dry up in the sun. And if the rain is very heavy it washes the saplings away." Another reason reforestation efforts have been only partially successful is that the slopes are too difficult to reach with replacement topsoil. The Chinese also place a low priority on maintaining the young seedlings.

Concerning Chinese use of Tibetan land, the Dalai Lama writes: "The conversion of marginal lands to agriculture for Chinese settlers has become the greatest threat to Tibet's grasslands. This has led to extensive desertification, rendering the land unusable for agriculture or grazing. The situation is made worse by fencing off grassland for horses and cattle, which has restricted the Tibetan nomads to ever smaller areas and disrupted their traditional migration practices."[15]

One of our interviewees was formerly a high-ranking lama, and had taken the oath of nonviolence. However, he looked forward to the day he could return to Tibet and join a campaign of guerrilla warfare to expel the Chinese. He said the occupiers were totally exploiting the land and killing massive numbers of animals. He related that in the earlier years of the occupation, the Tibetans' daily food supplies and basic necessities of survival were subject to their supplying the Chinese with a quota of small corpses, showing that they had killed unwanted "pests" which included birds, small mammals, and insects. The occupiers had little awareness of the role these small beings play in the ecological balance—thinking only that they might damage crops.

One of the monks reported a conversation he had with a high-ranking Chinese cadre member of the Communist Party, in May of 1989. Asking when the Chinese would return to their own country, he was told that, in a meeting at Dri-Du Dzong District, the district commissioner had stated, "We will leave Tibet only after we take out all of the trees and minerals, and dump all our atomic waste."

An interview was held with a young refugee who had recently fled to Dharamsala, India. He gave an example of how the Chinese offend the Tibetans' religious beliefs and harm the creatures living in the environment. Like other creatures of nature, fish are considered to be "sentient beings," possessing feeling and having a past and future. The young Tibetan had observed first hand how the Chinese fish in rivers, streams, and lakes: the Chinese fishermen drive the fish toward one edge of the lake and throw dynamite into the area. Fish, small and large, float to the top of the water, blown apart by the blast. No re-seeding of the water with minnows was observed. Another method is to put electrodes into the area where the fish have been trapped. A powerful electric current is sent across a gap stunning the fish, which float to the surface. They are brought to market in pails. The Tibetan observer noted that, not infrequently, Tibetans will buy the fish that have survived the shock and return them to their aquatic abode, where they swim out of harm's way, at least temporarily. Saving the fish is in keeping with the Tibetan respect for nature. The Tibetans have a saying: "Because a fish is without a tongue, killing is unforgivable."[16]

Keeping the concept of interdependence in mind, it is interesting to note that the killing off of Tibet's wild animals is also having an adverse effect on crop production. As herds of predatory animals have been killed off, populations of small animals such as moles, rabbits, marmots, and Tibetan pika have increased. As these herbivores have multiplied unchallenged, they have attacked and destroyed the root systems of grasses and grains. As fewer and fewer roots hold the soil, desertification is increasing.[17]

Tibetans believe the earth is sacred. Therefore, they traditionally avoided mining except for extracting small amounts of precious stones, gold, and silver, which they used to make sacred images and jewelry. They also traded small quantities with India and Nepal for tea and other items they were unable to obtain in Tibet. But this tradition of restraint, like so many others, died with the Chinese occupation.

With a diminishing supply of minerals, and a dependency upon supplies from abroad, China has been very pleased with their exploration into the mineral reserves in Tibet. They have located abundant supplies of copper, iron, chromate, lithium, and borax, just a few of the 126 minerals known to be found in Tibet. Apparently most of their discoveries have not been in the Tibetan Autonomous Region or Kham, but in Amdo.

Tibet has become a rich source of petroleum for the Chinese. In 1981, they discovered fifteen oil fields in the Qaidam Basin, in Amdo. These fields have produced an annual yield of approximately 7.5 million barrels of crude oil. These petroleum reserves are some of the most important ones under Chinese rule.

Although gold has long been mined in a minor way in Tibet, in 1989 the Chinese ran across a large deposit in the Tridu district in Amdo and began large-scale operations. As an example of the richness of the deposits, some farmers found one nugget that weighed almost eight pounds. Kham is also a region where remarkable concentrations of gold are being mined.

A thirty-six-year-old man who escaped to India from Derge in Kham, in 1989, told us about mining:

> The Chinese....are digging the earth for mineral resources, especially gold, silver and bronze, which are plentiful in my area.... All the people are aware that the land is being over-exploited by taking from our land all the available mineral resources. Many people have voiced their concern against the Chinese to stop the exploitation of gold and other resources.... The gold and all other resources are being taken to China for the development of China and not Tibet. If these minerals are used to develop Tibet, then it is tolerable.... The Chinese are, in fact, striking at the very root of our way of life.

Vast gold deposits have led to a gold rush in Amdo, where Chinese authorities have lost control over mining. Chinese farmers and city dwellers with gold rush fever flood into the area in hopes of striking it rich. These new settlers have created chaos. In addition to violence associated with the mad rush to get rich quickly, these settlers use small-scale hydrologic equipment, which has contributed to erosion in the area.[18]

The Chinese have discovered another resource in many areas of the plateau that may pose an even greater danger than depletion of gold and other minerals. That resource is uranium. The authorities kept information about it secret after its discovery in the 1960s, until 1993. They have also kept secret a nuclear research testing and production station called the Ninth Academy; it is located in the region of Lake Koko Nor, in a 1,170 square-kilometer forbidden zone immediately north of the Tibetan border. Details about the operation of the facility are sketchy. The Chinese claim to have moved the facility to a site in Sichuan Province, where they feel it would be less subject to attack.[19] For many years, Tibetans in the region have reported unusual numbers of people dying of cancer.[20]

Not only has China established a nuclear energy industry, the Chinese have offered Western nations the option of sending their nuclear waste to Tibet to be dumped at the cost of $1,500 per kilogram.[21] The intended dump site is a twenty-square-mile area located in the Haibei Autonomous Prefecture near the shores of Lake Koko Nor, in a disputed border area between China and Tibet.

China's willingness to provide a dump for nuclear wastes has alarmed environmentalists around the world. China has opened the gate to other types of toxic wastes as well. Greenpeace USA discovered documentation proving that China planned to accept a shipment of a half-million tons of sewage sludge from the city of Baltimore. The Chinese authorities intended to use the sludge, which was bound for Tibet, as fertilizer despite the fact that the sludge contained toxic household wastes.

The Chinese development policy has taken a terrible toll on Tibet. And, while the situation in cities such as Lhasa is dire, the effects of this policy can be seen in the countryside as well. Since the 1980s, China has sought money from abroad to further its major development projects, such as the Yamdrok Yumtso Lake Project. Started in 1990, this project is designed to create a source of electric power by linking the lake with the Lower Yarlung Tsangpo River, 2,700 feet below, by digging a tunnel. When the project is completed, water crashing through the tunnel will power generators at hydroelectric stations. Then, at night, the Chinese say water will be pumped back up the mountain to replenish the lake. However, Austrian and American contractors supervising the project scoff at this. They say that the Chinese will be "unwilling to sacrifice the huge amount of power needed to pump the water uphill."[22]

In August 1996, reports surfaced of a tunnel collapse in which about 1,000 cubic meters of rock fell, causing a major setback to the hydroelectric project. The collapse happened in September or October, 1995, and had been kept secret by the Chinese authorities. This setback will reportedly require the re-excavation of damaged sections, thus increasing the cost of the project from its original budget of $79 million to $236 million.[23]

Tibetans have protested vehemently against this project not only from the standpoint of potential environmental hazards, but also because they consider the lake to be especially sacred. The United Nations Development Program has questioned the environmental desirability and practicality of the project. Despite the strength of the protests and the substantial technical problems, work on the project continues. The original completion date was set for the year 2000. Austrian, Japanese, and American firms have contracted to supply the hydroelectric machinery and repair equipment for the project.

Namgyal, a young man from Kham who recently escaped to India, told us:

> The situation is getting worse. Life is becoming very difficult for both man and animals. The land has been dug out everywhere. In independent Tibet, there was a lot of wildlife, and these animals were protected by law as well as by religious teachings. These days, the Chinese kill and are still killing large numbers of them. When the lamas intervened and requested that the Chinese not kill the wildlife, the Chinese rebuked the lamas and told them not to interfere. They directed the lamas to mind their own business. Everything that is worthy from the land is being sucked out—the mineral resources, the forest resources, wildlife.... Even the grass won't grow as easily as before. Tibetans are facing cut-throat competition in getting employment in the face of the large influx of Chinese migrants. We don't have rights of movement like in the old days. Even things to eat are less under the Chinese.

Speaking to members of the U.S. Congress on September 21, 1987, the Dalai Lama said, "Prior to the Chinese invasion, Tibet was an unspoiled wilderness sanctuary in a unique natural environment." After forty years of occupation, Tibet can no longer be described as "an unspoiled wilderness."

Yaks were decorated with bright yarn as part of the religious observances held during planting season.

Shelters were built to provide protection for livestock during harsh weather. The walls were plastered with yak dung, a valued resource. Traditionally, semi-nomads, or farmers with substantial herds of livestock grazed their animals in high pastures during the summer, bringing them down to the village for winter.

Plowing a field in U-Tsang. Farmers fortunate enough to own livestock employ yaks to pull the plow.

Farmers bundling barley straw during the harvest. Children and infants partake in the activities (U-Tsang).

A farming family winnowing barley. Nomads depend upon farmers primarily for barley, while farmers depend upon nomads for a variety of products including meat, cheese, and butter.

Ganden Monastery, one of the oldest and largest in Tibet in the 1920's before its destruction by Chinese soldiers (U-Tsang).

Ganden Monastery following its destruction during the Cultural Revolution. Although parts were rebuilt, Ganden was closed in 1996 by the Chinese to punish the monks for having photographs of the Dalai Lama.

Ruins of the monastery at Tingrig, destroyed during the Cultural Revolution (U-Tsang).

During the Cultural Revolution, revered religious artifacts and icons were systematically destroyed or melted down and sent to China. These beautiful murals in the monastery at Samye were partially destroyed as the room was turned into a woodshed.

A familiar scene in traversing Tibet is the product of Chinese road building. This mountainside has been left totally bare, ripe for erosion and landslides.

A typical example of road blockage and silting resulting from a landslide caused by clearcutting, on the border between Tibet and China.

An example of damage caused by reckless clearcutting of Tibetan forests. It is estimated that approximately 50 percent of Tibet's forests have been cut down, with little or no attempt to restore the devastated land. Consequences include extensive erosion, flooding, and the silting of the many Asian rivers that arise in Tibet (Kham).

Although laws against the hunting of endangered species exist, the Chinese have shown no commitment to enforcing them, and the once abundant wildlife has largely disappeared. This snow leopard skin, hung up for sale on the open market, was photographed in Lhasa.

Near the Nepali border in the high mountains, Tibetan women are conscripted to carry 100-pound timbers to an area where they can be trucked out to China.

Steady streams of trucks have been observed carrying timber back to China.
One observer counted 50 trucks in one hour (Kham).

A group of elderly nomads and farmers who provided the authors with information on their former life in Tibet (Dharamsala, India).

The authorities in China are well aware of the environmental effects their policies are having in Tibet. In 1985, Wu Zhengyl, a researcher at the Kunming Institute of Botany in Kunming, China, observed that particularly in mountainous regions, "there is destruction of natural resources continuously creating more and more new problems: areas of soil erosion are increasing and the erosion is serious, the silting up of rivers, lakes and reservoirs is severe, and the mileage of inland navigation has been reduced."[24]

Nevertheless, the Chinese-sanctioned environmental destruction continues in Tibet, and along with the environment, a time honored, environmentally sound way of life is being destroyed.

NOTES

1. Kim Yeshi, "Tibetan Buddhist View of the Environment," *Chö-Yang* (Kuala Lampur, Malasia: Graphic Press, 1991), 264.
2. "Re-education Teams Sweep Tibetan Monasteries," *Tibet Press Watch* 9, no. 3 (July 1997): 1.
3. T. Danlock, "Tibet's Changing Ecology," *Essential Environmental Materials on Tibet* (Washington, D.C.: International Campaign for Tibet, 1990), 41.
4. Bradley Rowe and Clair Longrigg, *Deforestation in Western China and Tibet* (Washington, D.C.: International Campaign for Tibet, 1990), 17.
5. Tibet Environmental and Developmental Project Team, "Tibet Environmental and Developmental Issues," Department of Information and International Relations, Central Tibetan Administration, Dharamsala, India, 1992, 27.
6. Galen Rowell, "The Agony of Tibet," *Greenpeace* 15, no. 2 (Greenpeace USA, Washington, D.C., March/April 1990), 6.
7. "The State of Tibet's Environment," *Tibet Environment and Development News*, Washington, D.C., 1994, 10.
8. Rowell, "The Agony of Tibet," 10.
9. Tibet Environmental and Developmental Project Team, "Tibet Environmental and Development Issues," Department of Information and International Relations, Central Tibetan Administration, Dharamsala, India, 1992, 4.

10. Robbie Barnett, "Notes on the Environmental Crisis in Tibet," *Essential Environmental Materials on Tibet,* 2d ed. (Washington, D.C.: International Campaign for Tibet, 1990), 3.

11. Lolo Houbein, "Article on Logging in Kham," report submitted to Tibet World News via the Internet by Burlo@world.net and posted on September 5, 1995.

12. Gabriel Lafitte, "A Chinese Report on Deforestation in Tibet," *Tibetan Review,* March 1990.

13. Robbie Barnett, "Notes on the Environmental Crisis in Tibet," 3.

14. Elmer Reiter, "How Tibet's Climate Affects Other Countries," *Natural History* 90, no. 9 (1981), 11.

15. "The State of Tibet's Environment," *Annual Newsletter* (Washington, D.C.: International Campaign for Tibet, 1993-1994).

16. M. H. Duncan. *Love Songs and Proverbs of Tibet* (London: The Mitre Press, 1961), #441.

17. Bradley Rowe, "The Changing Ecology of the Tibetan Plateau," *Annual Newsletter* (Washington, D.C.: International Campaign for Tibet, 1993-1994).

18. "Gold Hunters, Defying Beijing, Mine Vast Areas of Rural China," *New York Times*, July 16, 1995, 1.

19. Xinhua News Report, July 1995.

20. "China Admits to Nuclear Waste on Tibetan Plateau," International Campaign for Tibet, August 15, 1995, issued via the Internet.

21. Tibet Environmental Development Team, "Tibet: Environmental Development Issues," Department of Information and International Relations, Central Tibetan Administration, Dharamsala, India, 1992, 60.

22. Eunice Kange, "The Hydropower Station at Yamdrok Tso Lake," *News Tibet,* May-August 1993, Office of Tibet, New York.

23. "Hydro-Electric Project: Tunnel Collapse," compiled by Tseten Samdup; *World Tibet Network News*, published on Internet by The Canada-Tibet Committee (wtn-editors@utcc.utoronto.ca), Issue ID: 96/08/11 20:15 GMT, archived at: http://www.omtanken.se/sve_tib/ wtnn.htm, 1996.

24. Wu Zhengyl, *The Management of Natural Resources in Drainage Areas*, International Centre for Integrated Mountain Development, 1985, 9.

CHAPTER SIX

Endangered Tibetans

"When people die, the next generation replaces them, but when a whole culture is destroyed it can never be replaced. Tibet has always been quite separate from China in religion, culture, and language. We have a right to be free and we are confident that we shall get our country back—maybe after many years."[1]

Although the Chinese occupation has had a devastating effect on the environment, its consequences have been even more serious for the Tibetan people. In some ways, the environmental damage represents the outer covering, which has been denuded, mined, and polluted. Beneath this outer layer lies the substance—the Tibetan people, who have endured for decades under the Chinese occupation. During our interviews, we learned about their emotional scars and their courage in fighting for their basic core values and for their homeland.

The impact of the Chinese invasion of Tibet can be divided into four phases: the occupation period (1950-1959), the entrenchment period (1960-1965), the Cultural Revolution period (1966-1976), and the "Responsibility" period (1977 to the present). The occupation marked the entry of Chinese troops into Tibet, and culminated in the flight of the Dalai Lama and thousands of other Tibetans into exile in India, in 1959. This was followed in the early 1960s by a period of uprisings with many casualties and the destruction of thousands of monasteries.

During the late 1950s and early 1960s, the Chinese began to impose rules designed to chip away at the Tibetans' Buddhist values and strip away their human rights as well as their cultural heritage. Throughout Tibet, the people resisted these drastic changes.

From the mid-1960s through the mid-1970s, the Cultural Revolution set in motion a time of chaos and terror for Tibetans. China's Red Guards assumed control of all religious activities and economic life, forcing collectivization on nomads and farmers. Although there was an initial rebellion from the Tibetan people, the Red Guards quickly crushed the opposition.[2] Finally, since the late 1970s, the "Responsibility" system has aimed to return the economic activities of nomads and farmers away from collectives and back to the individual households.

Although at first the Chinese government's policies seemed benign to the Tibetans, the officials' actions clearly contradicted their words. Namgyal, a farmer from U-Tsang, told us: "In the beginning, when the Chinese took over all the land, they said, 'Everyone is equal, there is no status difference, you will all have a nice life.' People noticed what the Chinese said was not exactly true. In fact, what they had done was gradually starting to identify items and land and prime areas and saying, 'All this belongs to the state.' And what was not of any importance to them, and small things, they distributed around saying, 'Now you can have this and that and you have a nice life.' "

Tibetans quickly learned that the Chinese officials intended to dictate their regulations and that Tibetans would not have much choice in the matter. As Namgyal recalled, "People were just told. 'You have this much land and you are probably going to have this much crop and you have to hand over this much to the state.' People had no say, no argument regarding it. They had to give it because that was the order."

The agony caused by these arbitrary and brutally enforced changes was compounded by the deaths of hundreds of thousands of Tibetans.[3] One of the Chinese authorities' goals after the occupation was to increase agricultural yields by eliminating the age-old methods of food production used in Tibet and adopting "modern" methods of production. Chinese agricultural practices imposed on Tibet between 1958 and 1961 were diametrically opposed to the traditional methods practiced by Tibetans for centuries. The major crop in most areas of Tibet prior to the Chinese occupation was barley, a grain that drained few nutrients from the thin soil on that high, barren plateau. But when the Chinese took over Tibet, their officials forced farmers to grow wheat, a crop that saps far more nutrients from the soil.

Beginning in 1959, changes in planting practices did result in a dramatic increase in production of wheat and barley grains. This increase was accompanied by rigid quotas imposed by the Chinese on grain production. The Chinese authorities began taking much of the grain Tibetans produced. They sent much of it to China, which was experiencing a critical food shortage, and diverted much of the remaining harvest to feed the growing Chinese population in Tibet. The period of abundant crops was short-lived, however. Nutrients were so depleted that crop yields declined drastically, resulting in the first famine ever known in Tibet…in "every corner in Tibet…Tibetans were starving to death by the thousands."[4] Describing the desperate need for food from 1960 to 1963, Namgyal told us: "People had to consume certain strange herbs from the forest because there was nothing else to eat, and after consuming certain plants, people really swelled up. Basically, the herbs were not for consumption, but since they didn't have anything, that was all they could eat."

When we spoke to Dazang, who was from a semi-nomadic family from Amdo, she mentioned that she had received two years of education, but struggled in school due to the great famine. "During that period," she told us, "many Chinese and Tibetan people died through starvation, and if one family had ten members, only four or five of them were alive and the rest of them died of starvation. So there are many stories like that. Everybody was so hungry that they did not have the strength to even take the dead bodies for cremation or burial."

In adult life, Dazang lived on the shores of Lake Kokonor, a dry region, where she worked in a small fruit stand. Dazang described a large plant run by the Chinese which is strictly off-limits and where, she was told, the Chinese make nuclear weapons. About four years before our interview, she and her family successfully escaped to India, a four-month trip during which they had to dodge the Chinese border guards.

By the mid 1960s, the Chinese authorities had forced the collectivization of city workers, farmers, and nomads. The possessions of many wealthier Tibetan nomads and farmers were expropriated. The Red Guards established communes, and the animals and household goods of nomads and farmers became the property of these collectives. The communes attempted to destroy the Tibetan family structure. During this period of hardship, the core of Tibetan cultural beliefs came under assault. Long-held values were ridiculed and any form of religious expression was forbidden. Government officials assigned each person specific tasks and compensated workers through a point system.

Chinese officials, along with Tibetans who supported them, quickly assumed positions of power in the villages and controlled every aspect of village life, from what people could wear to what they could own. During our interviews, we encountered antagonism toward Tibetans who supported the Chinese government's position. Tibetans were not allowed to wear their traditional Chuba clothes because the Chinese claimed they would damage the crops by dragging them on the ground; instead they had to wear trousers. Chinese officials also refused to hire many Tibetans for government posts, claiming they were either suspected "reactionaries" or because they were from land-holding families.

The Red Guards ran "struggle sessions," or *'thab 'dzings*, which amounted to political indoctrination sessions aimed at abolishing any Tibetan cultural identity. Many thousands of Tibetans were subjected to this form of brainwashing. Tibetans who sided with the Chinese were hailed as heroes and used for propaganda purposes by the Chinese media. Confessions by Tibetans who then promised to support the Chinese government were made public. Nomads and farmers who sided with the Chinese alienated themselves from other Tibetans. There was disdain toward Tibetans who were Chinese sympathizers, and in some ways these "struggle sessions" helped to unite Tibetans to maintain their fight for their values.

We learned about the direct impact of the Chinese occupation when we spoke to Dawa, a sixty-one-year-old farmer who lived near Lhasa. Dawa had experienced some of the worst of the occupation during the Cultural Revolution, and was very clear in describing the lengths to which the Chinese went to change the traditional methods of agriculture. Dawa and his family suffered tremendously through the "shaming sessions." He recalled that during these sessions, the Chinese told them: "Those who were found innocent, those who were the sufferers of the past, would now get a lot of important posts and benefits." Dawa said that "certain people got carried away and...things became very, very serious. That is how the Chinese were able to get people to accuse others of certain acts. And so many of them were persecuted or maybe even killed."

In 1976, when the Cultural Revolution ended and was replaced by the "Responsibility System," nomads and farmers regained some control and responsibility for production for their animals and fields. The early 1980s signaled the break-up of communes and the redistribution of livestock. Tibetans were again allowed to manage their own herds and grow their crops.

However, nomads and farmers continue to face restrictions such as "voluntary" quotas for products sold to the Chinese government, limits on the size of the yak herds, the requirement of permits for travel to certain regions, licenses and taxes for trading, and so on. The Responsibility System has returned to Tibetans a certain amount of personal freedom, yet there remains an underlying distrust of the Chinese government. Although some monasteries have been allowed to be rebuilt and nomads have regained some control over their production, there is a sense that these freedoms can be revoked at any point if the Chinese government deems it necessary. The result is continued tension and apprehension.

The farming practices of Tibetans had become dependent on petroleum-based fertilizers, which are expensive, not always available, detrimental for the soil, and have limited success in increasing production yields. "In the past, we used manure to enrich the soil," Dawa informed us. Before the famine, farmers were happy with the new artificial fertilizers because they increased yields. "But," he said, "crop yield was decreasing and the soil was getting very hard.... However, we had no choice but to use it. Tibetans cannot refuse to use it...The [artificial] fertilizer used to be cheap, but now it costs a lot." We asked Namgyal, a farmer who escaped from Tibet in 1991, whether Tibetans could complain about this to the Chinese. He said, "The authorities would accuse us of being anti-progress and making statements against the state."

Nomads and farmers were also required to pay taxes to the Chinese government for their use of the land, for owning animals, and for their animal products such as cheese, milk, and wool. In some cases, Tibetans paid their taxes by selling their animals, but the Chinese officials would place a low value on goods sold by Tibetans. As Dolma, a farmer from Amdo, told us, "If you sell the wool to other people you get lots of money, but the Chinese government doesn't pay much money for it...You have to pay a certain percentage of sheep and yak to the Chinese. You have to provide them with meat. So when you sell your yak and sheep to the Chinese for tax, then the payment you get from them is very low. As for grassland tax, you have to pay in cash and you also have to pay the tax for keeping your domestic animals, according to the number."

The need to meet production quotas and the influx of Chinese settlers has resulted in changes in the traditional uses of land. Karma,[5] a farmer from Amdo whom we interviewed after he crossed the border into Nepal, stated that, as Chinese settlers moved into his village, "they pushed the Tibetan farmers out. The Chinese took the most fertile land from the Tibetans...forcing Tibetan farmers to move into hilly areas that nomads were using. And then the nomads had to move to higher and more distant areas to graze their yaks and other animals." Karma told us he left Tibet because the Chinese had pushed him off his land.

A nomad named Yutok, from Kham, told us that in the early days before the Chinese arrived, nomads had "good places for grazing animals." However, nomads who were sympathetic to the Chinese government were given the most fertile pastures: "The good pastures are all given to these [Chinese-sponsored] nomads.... The meats, butter, hides, extra wool [also] go to the Chinese [for] consumption. We are given only second-class grassland for grazing our animals." Yutok also said he was permitted to keep only a few animals and the rest were confiscated by the Chinese authorities.

Looting of Tibet's wealth has been going on for decades at a government-sanctioned level as well as at an individual level. Purba, who was imprisoned by the Chinese for ten years when he objected to the arrest of his brother, talked about the long-term implications of this looting. "While I was in prison," he said, "there was a Chinese prison officer named Wong. He came to Tibet around 1959 or 1960. When he came, he had an empty handbag, his bedding, and nothing else. In 1985, when he returned to China, he took back three trucks carrying wooden doors, cupboards, the skins of animals, and so forth." This type of looting occurs on a large scale. Purba commented, "In Tibet, we have 6 million people; in China there are about 1 billion people. If each Chinese individual takes back three trucks, not counting what the Chinese government is taking away, what will be left in Tibet? We do not have to do any other calculation."

Until the 1950 occupation, Tibet had a stable population of approximately 6 million people. There was sufficient food, negligible unemployment, and little crime. And the carrying capacity of the land was adequate to meet the needs of its population. In stark contrast, the population of China has been growing continuously. With well over 1 billion people, land resources in China are inadequate to provide food and other natural resources.

From the beginning, it appeared that China's intent in taking over Tibet was to transfer a significant segment of its population onto the Tibetan Plateau. However, Chinese authorities refused to admit this until 1994, when an official announcement from Beijing confirmed its established policy of promoting Chinese migration to Tibet.[6] To facilitate this transfer, the Chinese have developed an extensive infrastructure in Tibet which includes a highway system, expanded food production, industry, and human services. They accomplished this by heavily utilizing the services of the Chinese army.

In recent years, Chinese civilians have poured into Tibet in search of economic opportunities. According to the International Campaign for Tibet, there are currently 6 million Tibetans living in Tibet, while there are 7.5 million Chinese, most of whom live in Kham and Amdo.[7] "In Lhasa alone," the Campaign says, "where the Tibetans are estimated at 60,000, there are now approximately 150,000 Chinese civilians and security forces."[8]

Since the early 1980s, there have been reports of forced sterilizations of Tibetan women. This has been regarded as an outflow of China's population control policy and specifically as a means of turning Tibetans into a minority group in their homeland. Dazang told us: "Tibetan women don't like the idea of birth control policy but the Chinese officials call them [to] meetings every day and they introduce the birth control policy...telling the Tibetan women that they should get sterilized. So...Tibetan women cannot oppose this birth control policy...the Chinese police came to Tibetan people's homes and took the women to the hospitals by force and then got them sterilized...after that they could not give birth to any children."

The lengths to which the Chinese Government went to achieve its sterilization program were described by a woman from Amdo, who reported:

> "When I was pregnant with my third child, Chinese officials came to my house many times to convince me to have an abortion. They told me that I was not allowed to have a third child and that I should go to the hospital when I was about 5 months pregnant to have an abortion injection. I became very frightened and decide[d] to leave my home until the baby was due. I was afraid I would be forced to have an abortion if I stayed at home. I went to stay with my mother in another village. During the months I stayed with my mother, the officials who had told me to get an abortion came to my home about 10 times. They asked my husband where I was. When he said that he didn't know where I was they slapped him in the face, kicked him, and beat him with sticks. They threatened to arrest him if he didn't tell them where I was and if I didn't turn up. They carried pistols and handcuffs.
>
> When the baby was due I went home. About one month after the delivery, the officials came to my house again and threatened that they would take away all of our possessions and arrest my husband.... They ordered me to come with them to hospital.... I was given an injection in my spine. It was meant to anesthetize me but, in fact, I could feel exactly what the doctors were doing. The operation was very painful. There were four beds in the surgery room. I saw with my own eyes how they injected pregnant women with very long needles. They injected the head of the baby with some kind of poison. Later these women had miscarriages in the hospital. I saw many foetuses in the toilets. I saw how they were eaten by dogs. The parents weren't allowed to keep the foe-

tus unless they paid the medical bill for the operation. The bills were so high that nobody could pay them."[9]

In Tibet, Chinese shops dominate the economy. Since most Tibetans do not speak Chinese well enough to obtain jobs in these businesses and lack marketable skills, unemployment, lassitude, and alcoholism have spread among Tibetans to a degree never known before. During the mid-1980s, the authors witnessed large numbers of stores selling cheap liquor in major town centers such as Lhasa. The impact of alcoholism was prevalent throughout the streets; drunken Tibetans were in evidence, occasionally in confrontation with the Chinese. The result has been a deterioration of the social fabric of the Tibetan community, with little hope for improvement.

Soon after the Chinese takeover in 1959, Tibetan school children were not allowed to learn the Tibetan language and instead were taught Chinese. Over the years, Chinese officials have placed a low priority on educating the next generation of Tibetans. The school system contributes to, rather than protects against, the marginalization of Tibetans. The illiteracy rate for Tibetans is three times higher than the rate for Chinese, partially because the school system is designed for those who already speak Chinese and, to a lesser degree, for those who are willing to learn Chinese. Most Tibetans are only permitted to attend schools designated for them. These schools place little emphasis on teaching them to read either Tibetan or Chinese. In addition, many of those Tibetans who wish to attend school have no opportunity. For example, in 1994, the Chinese reported that 120,000 school-age Tibetan children were not in school, and another 120,000 had to stand in class because there weren't any chairs or desks.[10]

In many respects, the situation faced by Tibetans is similar to that faced by the North American Indians in the past. Both groups have been displaced from their land and marginalized by a dominant society. Historically, Native Americans were relegated to reservations, where alcoholism and unemployment became rampant. Similarly, Tibetans are becoming peripheral in their own homeland to a new mainstream: the Chinese. The steady stream of Chinese moving to Tibet has become both an environmental and human rights problem. With the growing number of immigrants, the population could soon overload the carrying capacity of the land, furthering Tibet's slide toward environmental degradation.

The dramatic changes in population and food production in Tibet have had a palpable effect on the health of Tibetans. Unpublished studies done by the Save the Children Foundation, the Woodlands Mountain Institute, and other child health researchers, have shown that children's growth on the Tibetan Plateau falls significantly below international growth reference standards by the age of two.[11] "One study examined children in a wide range of locations in Tibet and found evidence of delayed growth, protein deficiency, rickets, and intestinal parasites. Official Peoples Republic of China statistics report a higher infant mortality rate in Tibet than in inland China. It is hypothesized that the changes in diet causing child malnutrition are related to changed agricultural patterns and the unavailability of foods traditionally obtained by barter between agricultural and nomadic groups.

A twenty-two-year-old Tibetan told us that all the adult members of his family were much taller than the members of his generation. This *samarog* family had suffered considerably from a lower standard of living following the confiscation of the family's agricultural and livestock resources. At times, his father had to steal food to keep the family alive. The continuation of this type of deprivation over a prolonged period can have a devastating effect on the future of the once hardy Tibetan population.

The Chinese have been successful in obtaining funds for community development projects in Tibet from a number of governmental and non-governmental organizations such as the United Nations and Wildlife Conservation International, among others. Most of these organizations have explicit guidelines requiring the involvement of local people in the economic development programs they fund. However, the Chinese have succeeded in convincing funding organizations that there is, in fact, local support for projects, but once the money is allocated, the foreign funding organizations have no control over the projects. One exception is the Panam project, which was subsequently terminated when its objectives were disclosed. The Panam project illustrates many of the pitfalls associated with Western-style development schemes designed by China in rural areas like Tibet.

In 1988, the European Union's (EU) Panam project was undertaken using funds from the United Nations' World Food Program. The project was designed to help alleviate poverty and improve socio-economic conditions for Tibetans living in the county of Panam, 200 kilometers southwest of Lhasa, by implementing Western-style high-yield agricultural methods, a medical program, and a Chinese education system.[12] The primary objective was to increase grain production but, in fact, this region of Tibet had a surplus of barley and wheat. Barley accounted for almost 80 percent of the crops grown in the region, and wheat, less than 5 percent. The project aimed to replace barley varieties with higher-yielding wheat monocultures. The new varieties, however, are more susceptible to pests and disease, and to a variety of natural hazards. There was no record of sustaining these higher yields in this region, which had been plagued by deforestation and overgrazing, and no environmental impact study had been undertaken to assess the potential effects of introducing new grain crops.

From an economic perspective, the Panam project would have replaced a barter system of trade with a cash-based system. Tibetans would become increasingly dependent on a credit system managed by Chinese banks. In effect, this economic shift would have affected every aspect of Tibetans' life by forcing them to abandon their subsistence economy and turn toward an uncertain market-oriented system, with no control over pricing and availability.

In essence, many of the objectives of the Panam project were misguided and reflected a lack of understanding of the ecology of the region and of the needs of the local Tibetan communities. Not only did a study by Cultural Survival find that the project planning was mismanaged, it found that there were "no clear indications that the project was born out of the wishes of local Tibetans, or that their interests have been addressed, or that they will have any real say in the design or decision-making processes of the project."[13] In February 1995, the European Commission (EC) suspended the Panam project for two years. In January 1997, a revised Panam project proposal was finalized, in which guarantees to local Tibetans as sole beneficiaries were eliminated, and non-governmental organizations were excluded from participation.[14]

This latest arrangement would hamper monitoring of benefits for Tibetans by excluding non-governmental workers' involvement.

The findings of Cultural Survival, a Massachusetts-based organization that conducted a survey of development projects in Tibet, showed that the projects did not have sufficient and adequate input from the Tibetan people. The survey also found that the projects lacked the necessary planning and consideration of local circumstances to ensure that the outcome would be in keeping with the cultural, social, and economic needs of Tibetans.[15] Cultural Survival surveyed international and non-profit organizations such as the United Nations, the United Nations International Children's Emergency Fund (UNICEF), the United Nations Development Programme (UNDP), the Red Cross, Médicins Sans Frontières, Save the Children, and Volunteers in Service of America. It also looked at projects initiated by the Chinese themselves.

In many ways, the disastrous effects of the Chinese government's development efforts in Tibet mirror many of the flaws of development schemes attempted elsewhere in developing regions of the world. Cultures such as that of Tibet, which have successfully practiced pastoralism and farming for thousands of years, have proven the efficacy of their techniques through the ages. Forcibly imposing new crops, fertilizers, and social structures under duress undoubtedly has a high chance of failing. And indeed, this has largely been the case.

One of the ways the Chinese government hopes to solidify its control of Tibet is through economic reforms. The objective involves attempting to diffuse popular unrest by improving the Tibetans' economic opportunities. This initiative has focused on luring nomads and farmers into an increasingly cash-based economy fueled from mainland China. The economic reforms have improved Tibetans' standard of living, but the oppressive regulations remain a roadblock. By reinstituting some of their traditional practices, nomads and farmers have become less dependent on Chinese goods and services. Tibetans in rural areas seem content living with their basic necessities and have not become overly dependent on the materialism of Western culture now gripping parts of China.

Another strategy adopted by the Chinese government has focused on increasing tourism as a way of launching Tibetan society into modernization. However, Western tourism has imported democratic ideals and a sympathetic attitude on the part of many visitors for the Tibetan fight for freedom and self-determination. Recently, the Chinese government has decided to control tourism as a way of minimizing the potential for political unrest. This is done by requiring visitors to travel in organized groups, and by keeping them from speaking to Tibetans. Tibetans who talk to foreigners risk arrest.

Nevertheless, the potential is there for the success of simple, development programs that would serve some of the isolated communities on the Tibetan Plateau. Using local economic resources, windmills, drip irrigation, and solar greenhouses could solve some of the problems faced by local residents. Proposals have looked at implementing agriculture demonstration projects, improving irrigation systems and drinking water, and introducing latrines requiring minimal amounts of water (See photo, p. 75). Additional plans include establishing wind-generated projects, solar water-heating systems, solar ovens, and bio-gas projects. The success of each of these programs often depends on the involvement of the local community in the planning and development phase as well as the ongoing financial, technical, and management commitment from the organization involved in the program.

Nomads and farmers may benefit from projects aimed at increasing their productivity without sacrificing their traditional social structure. Nomads, for example, may improve their livelihood through solar ovens and solar water-heating systems. Farmers may also benefit from bio-gas and irrigation projects for their fields. Ultimately, these programs will succeed only when they are fully embraced by the Tibetans and when the communities involved have a leading role in the design and implementation procedures.

In searching for a successful model where development projects have been embraced by the local culture, we have to look no further than to Ladakh, known as "Little Tibet." The kingdom of Ladakh, in northwest India, adjoins western Tibet and has a similar environment characterized by high altitude and an arid climate. Ladakh also has very close cultural and historical ties to Tibet.

Western organizations, including the International Society for Ecology & Culture (ISEC)[16], have been working closely with the local villagers and the Indian government to establish development projects that empower local communities. Irrigation, energy, and agricultural projects run by local officials trained by Western organizations have provided the tools and techniques for solving some of these problems. The result has been a lasting commitment to finding simple, low-cost, efficient solutions that rely on local resources. And most importantly, the involvement of the local people has generated the support required to make these programs viable.

The resilience and hard-earned survival of the Tibetan people is an example for other indigenous cultures of the determination to withstand total annihilation by an occupying force. The Tibetan culture remains endangered by a continuing onslought of Chinese-style development schemes. Tibet remains at a crossroads, with the Tibetans attempting to maintain their cultural identity in the midst of the tumultuous change presently occurring in China. Nevertheless, the spread of Tibet support groups internationally has shed light on some exciting opportunities for a positive outcome of the Tibetan situation. We must remain optimistic about a mutually beneficial solution to the issue of Tibet since the loss of the Tibetan culture would have repercussions far beyond the Tibetan Plateau. In the final chapter, we will examine what is at stake for Tibetans and for the world.

NOTES

1. Rinchen Dolma Taring, *Daughter of Tibet* (New Delhi: Allied Publishers Private Ltd), 272.
2. The impact of the Chinese invasion on Tibet's people and culture, including their human rights record, has been extensively covered by other works. For a historical account of the Chinese occupation period through the early 1980s see: Avedon, John F., *In Exile from the Land of Snows* (New York: Vintage Books, 1984). For additional information on human the rights record, refer to the annotated bibliography.
3. Please refer to the bibliography for sources regarding the Chinese human rights record in Tibet.

4. John F. Avedon, *In Exile from the Land of Snows*, 237.
5. Karma had reached Nepal on his flight from Tibet the day before we interviewed him at the Tibetan Reception Center in Kathmandu.
6. "China Admits to Policy of Promoting Chinese Migration to Tibet," *Tibetan Environment and Development News*, Washington, D.C., no. 15, 1. 1995.
7. International Campaign for Tibet, *Tibet at a Glance . . .*, (fact sheet), Washington, D.C.
8. International Campaign for Tibet, *Tibet Transformed: A Pictorial Essay Documenting China's Colonization of Tibet*, Washington, D.C., 1994, 5.
9. Tibetan Women's Association, "Tears of Silence," *Tibetan Women and Population Control 39* (1994) (interview with "C," a Tibetan woman from Amdo, conducted in India in April 1994).
10. Teresa Poole, "Paying the Price of Progress," *The Independent* (London), August 20, 1995. Please note that these figures apply only to the TAR (Tibet Autonomous Region) and do not include the provinces of Amdo and Kham, which China has annexed into its western provinces.
11. Personal communication with author.
12. *Tibet Information Network* (TIN) News Review, no. 23, London, March 1995, 29.
13. *Tibet Information Network* (TIN) News Review, no. 23, London, March 1995, 28.
14. *Free Tibet Campaign*, London, Press Release, January 21, 1997.
15. Ann Forbes and Carole McGranahan, "Developing Tibet? A Survey of International Development Projects," *Cultural Survival Report no. 33* (Washington, D.C.: The International Campaign for Tibet, May 1992), 117.
16. For more information on community development projects in Ladakh contact: International Society for Ecology and Culture (ISEC), P.O. Box 9475, Berkeley, CA 94709, USA.

CHAPTER SEVEN

Tibet As a Living Model

"I have proposed that all of Tibet become a sanctuary, a zone of peace. Tibet was that once, but with no official designation. Peace means harmony: harmony between people, between people and animals, between sentient beings and the environment."
—*His Holiness the 14th Dalai Lama*[1]

In this work, we have attempted to shed light on the unique aspects of the Tibetan culture and its importance for the survival of all peoples on earth. We examined some attributes of Tibetan society through accounts of their daily lives by nomads and farmers. Our aim was not to romanticize their lives, nor in any way to paint Tibet as a one-time Shangri-La. Rather, we have tried to show how these rugged pastoralists and tillers of the soil managed to cope on a land that one would think could not support a desirable lifestyle. As we learned from our interviews with nomads, farmers, monks, and former monks, the quality of life achieved, as seen by them, provided ample resources and gratification. The fine-tuning they accomplished in adjusting to the vagaries of the weather, wildlife, and soil conditions seems to us nothing short of remarkable. Measured by their own standards, and influenced by Buddhism, they experienced both equanimity and a palpable sense of freedom.

During our conversations, we reviewed the ecological wisdom nomads and farmers acquired through devising effective survival strategies that were passed from generation to generation without depleting nature's bounties. As we learned about these ecological practices, we acknowledged that they have been successfully implemented for thousands of years—and have been woven into Tibetans' daily responsibilities almost as second nature. We have also noticed the Tibetans' active engagement with appreciation of the natural world that surrounds them.

As we revisit the issue, "Why care about Tibet?", we see that Tibetans stand at a critical juncture in history. Tibetans may become a casualty of China's modern development process, remaining a fragmented and disappearing ethnic minority, or they may regain their independence and serve as a beam of hope for the world, as a culture with an immense spiritual abundance and an earth-based wisdom. The choices at hand mark an unprecedented opportunity for a winning solution that would benefit all nations.

Prospects for Tibet under the Chinese

What is the significance of the losses as the occupation continues? At present, without any major shift in the Chinese policy, it is realistic to anticipate an ever-increasing deterioration in Tibet's situation. This path will affect the lives of the people, the survival of their culture, and the health of the environment. It is important to appraise the nature of the loss, not only for the Tibetan people but for the world at large.

Clearly, the Tibetan culture is a seminal one carrying within it priceless knowledge, cultural heirlooms, in effect, that can teach us how to survive satisfactorily in a place where abundance is rare or unknown and where the shifting forces of nature can be cruel and unforgiving. The incremental demise of this distinct group of people depletes the world's reservoir of enduring wisdom—a wisdom available to serve the world as a beacon in its global environmental crises. The keen ecological insights derived from millennia of stewardship over their land would be lost. The *environmental ethic* the Tibetans have developed, in which human beings live in harmony with nature, would be gone but might be described somewhere in a chapter on the past history of Tibet. By trying to rescue the Tibetans, we may indeed be rescuing ourselves!

Should Tibetans survive their crisis, their unmatched knowledge and values could be of great benefit as the world becomes more populous and has fewer resources on which to depend. Survival of this heritage can best be achieved by assuring that the Tibetan people live and work on their own land. For the world to stand by and watch Tibetan society being decimated through cultural genocide is indefensible. A demoralized society under an egregious occupation cannot hold onto its heritage forever.

Although Tibetans make up only .05% of China's population, almost 25% of China is labeled as the "Tibetan Autonomous Region (TAR)." Only about half of official Tibet lies in the TAR, which accounts for less than half of the Tibetan people. The rest has been assimilated into four Chinese provinces. A report by Steven D. Marshall and Susette Ternent Cooke of the Alliance for Research in Tibet (ART) states: "China's presence and behavior in Tibetan areas can be distilled to three fundamentals: control, exploitation, assimilation." In addition, these findings "...are striking in that they are *conspicuous* in every seat of administrative control, *consistent* throughout centers of control and *impactful* in all areas controlled."[2]

The long-range effects of the continuation of the environmental assault and degradation set into motion by the Chinese are incalculable. Pollution of the rivers and streams, further desertification of the land, denuding of the forest, loss of diversity among plant and animal life, and the threat to the physical health of the people have already had a devastating impact. With massive development in the Tsangpo valley, air pollution will envelop Lhasa and the Potala. If Chinese exploitation continues, damage caused by the silting and flooding of Asia's principal rivers flowing out of Tibet will become acute. The Tibetans liken this complex river system to the arteries in the body. With the rivers flowing normally, health is maintained; however, if the water, like blood, becomes contaminated or impure, famine and hardship would ensue. The rice-growing countries to the south and down-river would be particularly vulnerable. In essence, the effects of these changes have become a global issue, not merely a regional one.

Especially troublesome would be the impact on global politics. The inability and impotence of international world bodies to confront China effectively on the issues —cultural genocide, human rights, environmental deterioration, and massive population transfers in Tibet—are already apparent. The attempts of sovereign nations, as well as non-governmental organizations, to challenge China's controlling influence in the United Nations have often been unsuccessful. China continues to use the "carrot and stick" strategy to coerce its client states and trading partners. Individual nations are often seduced by the benefits of lucrative commercial contracts offered by China as an incentive for political support. This outcome weakens the ability to take a firm stand in the United Nations and act on global hazards in Tibet and elsewhere in the world. The United Nations' willingness and strength to assume responsibility in Tibet may be a bellwether for how the world will deal with other major environmental problems of international significance.

A Ray of Optimism

Since the invasion in the 1950s, China's overwhelming impact on Tibet and its people, and the lack of international support, have generated considerable pessimism for the future both inside and outside Tibet. This pessimism can ferment and turn into depression and apathy. Eventually, this apathy could be a death knell for a people stripped of their culture and their future.

Fortunately, defeatism has gained little ground due to the efforts of the pro-Tibet movement and political action groups from around the world. In increasing numbers, grassroots organizations are gathering momentum to support the cause of the Tibetan people and to protest the destruction of their native environment. Efforts in Europe, North America, New Zealand, and Australia have been geared to educate the public on the essential facts and issues surrounding Tibet's plight. As a result, the understanding of Tibet's situation is considerably greater today than at the time of the initial invasion.

The nonviolent path Tibetans have followed has taken on a larger meaning recognized by many societies and governments. The accumulated good-will generated by His Holiness the Dalai Lama in his perpetual networking from country to country around the world with his message of nonviolence and respect for the environment, has gained the world's admiration, as evidenced by his receiving the Nobel Peace Prize in 1989.

At the national government level, parliamentarians in numerous countries and the leadership of many international organizations are increasingly speaking out against the wholesale violation of the human rights and environmental rights of Tibetans. The International Conferences on the Environment in Rio De Janeiro (1992) and New York (1997), The Human Welfare Conference in Copenhagen (1994), the Women's Conference in Beijing (1995), and the Habitat Conference in Istanbul (1996) have proved effective in broadening the understanding of the Tibetan problem. In these major conferences, China has blocked the official participation of His Holiness the Dalai Lama and the Tibet support groups (See Appendix D). As a consequence, their appearance on the scene as outsiders has made a major impact and gained recognition. Compared to the past, fewer countries are now willing to cave in to China's insistence on the status quo with Tibet; and they also are less likely to remain silent regarding China's punitive occupation and colonization practices.

The European Parliament has recognized and criticized the duplicity of China in its role in Tibet. It has taken a firm stand challenging the funding of Chinese-sponsored development projects in Tibet, particularly those that harm the environment, violate human rights, and only serve the expansionist needs of the Chinese people. The Congress of the United States recognizes Tibet as an independent country, and consistently condemns China's human rights abuses. Unfortunately, as a powerful trading partner China wields economic influence that is still strong enough to overcome national sentiments favoring human rights over commercial interests.

The International Commission of Jurists (ICJ), based in Geneva, released a report, *Tibet: Human Rights and Rule of Law*, in December, 1997, calling for a United Nations-sponsored referendum in Tibet on whether to remain under Chinese rule.[3]

Is China's hold on Tibet immutable? What alternative examples or scenarios can we envision that would provide a better outcome of the future? The dramatic changes and unexpected transitions that have taken place over the past five years in Eastern European countries, including the former Soviet Union, may foreshadow what will happen in China. National states such as Tajikistan, Kazakhstan, and Kirgizia, which had no previous autonomy, now exist in Central Asia. Countries whose boundaries, population, and heritage had never previously known independent statehood have recently become nations, free to work out their own destinies. Is it too far-fetched to believe this could happen in Tibet and the other regional minorities now under Chinese domination, such as Chinese Turkestan?

A Different Type of Development

Before the Chinese occupation, Tibet was a poor, non-democratic, third-world society. Progressive Tibetans realized by the 1940s that fundamental change was necessary. The Chinese invasion gave them no chance to evolve in their own way as a modern country. In the past fifty years industrial development has been adopted as a panacea for improving the economic status of third world countries with traditional rural economies and rich natural resources. Similarly, China's goal in the occupation of Tibet has been to promote rapid development, with all the infrastructure that accompanies it.

Experiences in every continent have shown that the abandonment of traditional rural agricultural systems and economies in exchange for urban industrial economies has created cities with vastly overpopulated slums, poverty, and unemployment. Crowded shanty towns, pollution, and disease are prevalent, and there is a breakdown of traditional rural farming skills. Although the status, "underdeveloped country," is often regarded as a negative condition to overcome, one must ask the question: *Development for what and for whom?* For Tibetans, "development," as they have experienced it, has become a synonym for oppression, greed, and exploitation.

Wisdom must question the notion of unrestrained expansion of the economy through industrialization. Development without consideration of how the changes will affect the people and the culture in the long run creates as many problems as it solves. Experience has shown that desirable development requires implementing changes that coincide with the goals of an informed and involved population. The full range of consequences needs to be predetermined and dealt with, if possible. Resources need to be renewable and changes must not endanger the environment. In this definition, a society's way of life can continue in balance because it neither uses up irreplaceable resources nor dishonors the environment. Such an approach would enhance Tibet's chances for a continued healthy existence.

The Tibetan Gift

For Westerners, it has become easier to understand the Tibetans' unique long-term survival, up until now, through their adherence to the basic laws of nature—what we call "ecology." Perhaps equally important, but less understood and appreciated, is the Tibetans' traditional goal of self-betterment. Acquired through meditation and embracing basic principles of existence, it is a means of addressing the common problems of living. From Buddha's own life experience and his observations concerning the prevention and alleviation of human suffering, a unique psychology took root. What gradually emerged is an inward-looking nonviolent culture based upon his teachings.

Terms like "medieval" and "archaic" have been applied to the Tibetan culture as it was before the occupation. However, these terms do not apply since Tibet was a different order of society than those of the West. In the West, civilization has gone through several phases of development: from our former feudal system, through the renaissance, the industrial revolution, to modernity today. Similarly, Tibetan civilization has progressively evolved from its archaic past at a different pace, using spiritual development as the focus of its value system.

It is very difficult to place a monetary value on the knowledge and wisdom of the Tibetan people. Undoubtedly, the Chinese have been able to reap monetary rewards from the mineral and forestry resources of Tibet. Yet, how do we ascertain the value of a culture? The answer lies in first examining the rights of all living things. Perhaps we should look at the intrinsic value of other cultures. Our appreciation increases as we become more knowledgeable about them, and we can begin to see that their right to exist and flourish is equal to ours in the industrialized countries.

Up until the seventeenth century, Tibet was a rather bellicose, militaristic country. Under the Fifth Dalai Lama—The Great Fifth as he is called—and subsequently, the monasteries increased their power over the military leadership and feudal landlords and became the dominant force. Monasteries, as we have seen, were to become more like educational institutions than sanctuaries for withdrawal from society. Directing the spiritual life of the Tibetan people, both rural and urban, they became the dominating influence. In contrast to social change in the West where "outer modernity" is the principle influence (espousing secularism, materialism, cosmopolitanism, technology, economic growth, and so on), the Tibetan Buddhist dogma stresses what Professor Robert Thurman calls "inner modernity." According to Professor Thurman, Tibet's "modernity is her conquest of the realms of the individual mind through a refined technology of self-perfecting education and contemplation. . . ."[4]

Having been an ordained monk in the Tibetan tradition himself, Professor Thurman brings an understanding of Tibetan teachings that illuminates for us the matchless quality of the Tibetan culture. He regards it as a source for learning that is imperative to achieve in order to survive in a world that has become unable to deal with rapid change and environmental catastrophes. In asking, "Why care about Tibet?," it is the preservation of this knowledge and these attributes that the culture *still* embodies that is essential—the cultural seeds, if you will, that must persevere to guide humanity through the trials of the present, and those sure to come in the future.

Historically, the nomads' life experience provides accumulated knowledge, amassed over thousands of years—a cultural equivalent to the DNA of the earth's human gene pool. In a similar fashion to the human genetic code, nomads and farmers retain an important strand of the earth's DNA-like cultural heritage. They embody a cultural library of knowledge and practical experience in living with the land. Their knowledge and expertise in areas such as animal husbandry, herbal medicine, spiritual practices, and socio-economic structures provide a wealth of wisdom. More importantly, nomads and farmers, like other indigenous peoples, form an essential aspect of the fabric of the human experience. The extinction of nomad and farmer societies would result in a great loss of the earth-based wisdom of a people rooted in a tradition of successful coexistence with the natural world.

A New Vision

The global agenda for the twenty-first century requires a new vision for changes affecting the human species—a principled, *environmental ethic* that embodies respect and appreciation for diversity in nature, and incorporates change that improves rather than diminishes the chances for subsequent generations. It would value native wisdom, recognizing that it can be taught to us by people from indigenous cultures such as Tibet and by other native peoples whose cultures have survived by living in harmony with nature.

In order to achieve this new vision, human beings need to stop thinking of themselves as being at the apex of the natural world and, instead, view themselves as responsible players in nature. The relationship between human beings and their environment would require that neither nature nor mankind be the loser. Mankind must shift from a dominant role to a cooperative one whereby we would recognize our interdependence with the environment. We would understand the subtle relationships between humans, wildlife, plants, and physical phenomena. Our views would shift from a mechanistic world-view to a holistic perspective based on understanding and respecting the living systems we all depend upon for our survival.

Tibet may serve as a model for maintaining traditional cultural identity while embracing change. In the business arena, this model can manifest itself through a private partnership with government institutions that support ecologically wise production methods. In agriculture, sustainable organic farming practices that have been utilized for hundreds of years would be reintroduced. For teaching the upcoming generation of Tibetan children, an educational program which stresses Tibetan cultural heritage and language would become the standard approach. The Tibetan Government-In-Exile in Dharamsala, India, has formulated a series of guidelines which would greatly ease the transition and implementation of such programs (See Appendix C).

Given the knowledge, energy, and resources of the Tibetans, we maintain the vision of a time that allows for the return of the country into the hands of its own people and, hopefully, the return of the Chinese immigrants to their own country. This resolution, of course, requires a reversal of China's devastating policies in Tibet, and protection, support, and assistance from the international community. Is it too much to expect that an ecosystem now in crisis can be healed and restored by its own indigenous population? Perhaps a culture such as this, when replanted in its natural environment, would bloom again.

A Zone of Peace

Tibet's will and drive for independence have been unshakable since the occupation in 1949. Looking toward independence, His Holiness the Dalai Lama has proposed that Tibet be transformed into a "Zone of Peace." As a completely demilitarized nuclear-free zone, it would serve as a buffer between India and China, formerly long-term foes. Intrinsic to this vision is a fully democratic nation dedicated to peace. It would fulfill its historical role of neutrality. The inhabitants would be masters of their own fate. An intensive effort would be needed to reverse the massive environmental damage brought about by the occupation. Wherever possible, the land and wildlife would be rehabilitated to their previous state.

A "Zone of Peace" is not a new concept. For thousands of years, places of worship have been established as sanctuaries and protected from outside infringement. In 1972, the United Nations Educational, Scientific, and Cultural Organization

(UNESCO) adopted the Convention Concerning World Cultural and Natural Heritage with a world-wide mandate to define sites of natural and cultural heritage. The notion is that their protection is the responsibility of the world. The Potala Palace in Lhasa has already been designated as such a site. Why not all of Tibet?

The Dalai Lama's vision of transforming all of Tibet into a Zone of Peace is an extension of this concept. It would be a precedent and a challenge for the world. A free, neutral Tibet could serve as a real living laboratory. It would be available to other countries to observe the progress in returning to or reaching sustainable development, the rehabilitation of the environment, and the experience of reintroducing or restocking endangered species. Recent scientific knowledge on the preservation and repopulation of endangered species could be effectively demonstrated in a large-scale environment such as Tibet. In accomplishing this goal, it could be an invaluable model to be replicated for regions in both hemispheres with endangered populations and damaged ecological areas. Support from public and private organizations would provide an unprecedented opportunity to the world to view positive environmental education and change in action.

Students from abroad could observe the process and participate in the revitalization of the ecosystem—returning Tibet to a healthy equilibrium. The mountains would be reforested. Endangered plant and animal species would be protected. Traditional methods of herding, agriculture, and collecting of medicinal herbs would be again practiced. Many social problems now seen in Tibet, including unemployment, apathy, and social malaise would be mitigated by full employment, as Tibetans again fashioned their own society.

The Tibetan Government-In-Exile's guidelines for future development (See Appendix C) urge that environmental and industrial development projects be of small scale and compatible with improving the quality of life. Sustainable technologies, not only for the present Tibetan generation but also to meet the needs of future generations, would be implemented. The teaching of Tibetan in schools would be reinstated. The principle in development would be "for and by the people of Tibet." Projects planned by the people, developed by the people, and operated by the people, would do much to reverse the spiral of alienation and despair. Many forms of technology that have been successfully demonstrated elsewhere could be introduced into Tibet.

During its period in exile, the Tibetan leadership has been keenly aware of the need to transform the culture and the governance into one more akin to Western-style democracies. Aware of previous shortcomings, the Tibetan Government-In-Exile has organized itself along democratic lines, with a representative government and elected parliament. The community of exiles in Dharamsala has taken the responsibility of educating itself so that once it returns it will have the knowledge and skills to function in an effective and responsible manner. Tibetans who have immigrated to Western-oriented countries are working and studying to develop aptitudes and skills in a full range of disciplines. Unlike most other immigrants, they wish, when it is feasible, to return to and contribute to their native land.[5]

Effective change requires a personal commitment. As His Holiness the Dalai Lama states, "I believe that every individual has a responsibility to help guide our global family in the right direction. Good wishes alone are not enough; we have to assume responsibility. Large human movements spring from individual human initiatives."[6] Individual efforts have made a tremendous difference in the social justice, peace, and environmental movements. Now, Tibet stands before us as an opportunity filled with hope. Through personal commitment and worldwide understanding, Tibetans can once again thrive in the Land of Snows.

NOTES

1. Tenzin Gyatso, The 14th Dalai Lama and Galen Rowell, *My Tibet* (Mountain Light Press, 1990): 80.
2. Steven D. Marshall and Susette Ternent Cooke, The Alliance for Research in Tibet (ART), *Tibet Outside the TAR: Control, Exploitation and Assimilation; Development with Chinese Characteristics*. Distributed as a CD-ROM available from International Campagn for Tibet (ICT), 1825 K Street NW, Suite 520, Washington D.C. 20006, 1997, 5-7.
3. "Jurists Call for Referendum on Status of Tibet (Tibet Bureau)," compiled by Thubten (Sam) Samdup, *World Tibet Network News*, published on Internet by The Canada-Tibet Committee (wtn-editors@utcc.utoronto.ca), Issue ID: 97/12/23, archived at: http:www.tibet.ca.
4. Robert A. F. Thurman, Sumner Carnahan, and Lama Kunga Rimpoche, *In the Presence of My Enemies* (Santa Fe, N.M.: Clear Light Publishers, 1995), xvii.
5. During our interviews, Tibetans expressed an overwhelming desire to return to their homeland.
6. The Dalai Lama, *Tibetan Review*, August, 1992, 20.

EPILOGUE

The Sheltering Tree of Interdependence

A Buddhist Monk's Reflections on Ecological Responsibility

The XIVth Dalai Lama

1 *O Lord Tathagata*
born of the Iksvakus
Peerless One
Who, seeing the all-pervasive nature
Of interdependence
Between the environment and sentient beings
Samsara and Nirvana
Moving and unmoving
Teaches the world out of compassion

2 *O the Savior*
The One called Avalokitesvara
Personifying the body of compassion
Of all Buddhas
We beseech thee to make our spirits ripen
And fructify to observe reality
Bereft of illusion

3 *Our obdurate egocentricity*
Ingrained in our minds
Since beginningless time
Contaminates, defiles, and pollutes
The environment
Created by the common karma
Of all sentient beings

4 *Lakes and ponds have lost*
Their clarity, their coolness
The atmosphere is poisoned
Nature's celestial canopy in the fiery firmament
Has burst asunder
And sentient beings suffer diseases
Unknown before

5 *Perennial-snow mountains, resplendent in their glory*
Bow down and melt into water
The majestic oceans lose their ageless equilibrium
And inundate islands

6 *The dangers of fire, water, and wind are limitless*
Sweltering heat dries up our lush forests
Lashing our world with unprecedented storms
And the oceans surrender their salt to the elements

7 *Though people lack not wealth*
They cannot afford to breathe clean air
Rain and streams cleanse not
But remain inert and powerless liquids

8 *Human beings*
And countless beings
That inhabit water and land
Reel under the yoke of physical pain
Caused by malevolent diseases
Their minds are dulled
With sloth, stupor, and ignorance
The joys of the body and spirit
Are far, far away

9 *We needlessly pollute*
The fair bosom of our mother earth
Rip out her trees to feed our short-sighted greed
Turning our fertile earth into sterile desert

10 *The interdependent nature*
Of the external environment
And people's inward nature
Described in the Tantras
Works on Medicine, and astronomy
Has verily been vindicated
By our present experience

11 *The earth is home to living beings;*
Equal and impartial to the moving and unmoving
Thus spoke the Buddha in truthful voice
With the great earth for witness

12 *As a noble being recognizes the kindness*
Of a sentient mother

And makes recompense for it
So the earth, the universal mother
Which nurtures all equally
Should be regarded with affection and care

13 *Forsake wastage*
Pollute not the clean, clear nature
Of the four elements
And destroy the well being of people
But absorb yourself in actions
That are beneficial to all

14 *Under a tree was the great Sage Buddha born*
Under a tree he overcame passion
And obtained enlightenment
Under two trees did he pass in Nirvana
Verily, the Buddha held the tree in great esteem

15 *Here, where Manjusri's emanation*
Lama Tson Khapa's body bloomed forth
Is marked by a sandalwood tree
Bearing a hundred thousand images of the Buddha

16 *Is it not well known*
That some transcendental deities
Eminent local deities and spirits
Make their abode in trees?

17 *Flourishing trees clean the wind*
Help us breathe the sustaining air of life

They please the eye and soothe the mind
Their shade makes a welcome resting place

18 *In Vinaya, the Buddha taught monks*
To care for tender trees
From this, we learn the virtue
Of planting, of nurturing trees

19 *The Buddha forbade monks to cut*
Cause others to cut living plants
Destroy seeds or defile the fresh green grass
Should not this inspire us
To love and protect our environment?

20 *They say, in the celestial realms*
The trees emanate
The Buddha's blessings
And echo the sound
Of basic Buddhist doctrines
Like impermanence

21 *It is trees that bring rain*
Trees that hold the essence of the soil
Kalpa-Taru, the tree of wish fulfillment
Virtually resides on earth
To serve all purposes

22 *In times of yore*
Our forbears ate the fruits of the trees
Wore their leaves

Discovered fire by attrition of wood
Took refuge amidst the foliage of trees
When they encountered danger

23 *Even in this age of science*
Of technology
Trees provide us shelter
The chairs we sit in
The beds we lie on
When the heart is ablaze
With the fire of anger
Fueled by wrangling
Trees bring refreshing, welcome coolness

24 *In the tree lie the roots*
Of all life on earth
When it vanishes
The land exemplified by the name
Of the Jambu tree
Will remain no more
Than a dreary, desolate desert

25 *Nothing is dearer to the living than life*
Recognising this, in Vinaya rules
The Buddha lays down prohibitions
Like the use of water with living creatures

26 *In the remoteness of the Himalayas*
In the days of yore, the land of Tibet
Observed a ban on hunting, on fishing

And, during designated periods, even construction
These traditions are noble
For they preserve and cherish
The lives of humble, helpless, defenseless creatures

27 *Playing with the lives of beings*
without sensitivity or hesitation
As the act of hunting or fishing for sport
Is an act of heedless, needless violence
A violation of the solemn rights
Of all living beings

28 *Being attentive to the nature*
Of interdependence of all creatures
Both animate and inanimate
One should never slacken in one's efforts
To persevere and conserve nature's energy

29 *On a certain day, month, and year*
One should observe the ceremony
Of tree planting
Thus, one fulfills one's responsibilities
Serves one's fellow beings
Which not only brings one happiness
But benefits all

30 *May the force of observing that which is right*
And abstinence from wrong practices and evil deeds
Nourish and augment the prosperity of the world
May it invigorate living beings and help them blossom

May sylvan joy and pristine happiness
Ever increase, ever spread and encompass all that is

During the course of my extensive traveling to countries across the world, rich and poor, east and west, I have seen people reveling in pleasure, and people suffering. The advancement of science and technology seems to have achieved little more than linear, numerical improvement; development often means little more than more mansions in more cities. As a result, the ecological balance—the very basis of our life on earth—has been greatly affected.

On the other hand, in days gone by, the people of Tibet lived a happy life, untroubled by pollution, in natural conditions. Today, all over the world, including Tibet, ecological degradation is fast overtaking us. I am wholly convinced that, if all of us do not make a concerted effort, with a sense of universal responsibility, we will see the gradual breakdown of the fragile ecosystems that support us, resulting in an irreversible and irrevocable degradation of our planet, Earth.

These stanzas have been composed to underline my deep concern, and to call upon all concerned people to make continued efforts to reverse and remedy the degradation of our environment. The poem is being released on the occasion of the presentation of a statue of Buddha to the people of India; and to mark the opening of the International Conference on Ecological Responsibility: A Dialogue with Buddhism.

Bhikshu Tenzin Gyatso
The XIVth Dalai Lama

APPENDIX A

Background of Tibet: Enduring Spirit, Exploited Land

It was in the mid 1980s that, following separate paths, we began our personal exploration of Tibet. We visited monasteries and temples and stopped to talk to nomads in their tent encampments. We stopped to look at farms and small villages as we journeyed across the ever-changing landscape of the Land of Snows. One of us traveled by a rickety Land Rover, the other bicycled the unpaved back-country, traversed mainly by nomads. We came to appreciate the hardiness and commitment to their unique lifestyle. We witnessed the exploitation of the Tibetan people by the foreign occupiers, observing the reckless manner in which their land was being voraciously degraded for greedy purposes, for another people in another country. Returning home, we found others who had visited Tibet and had become committed to taking action in behalf of the Tibetan people.

During this period (1985-1990), more reports were coming out of Tibet from fleeing refugees, and also from foreign tourists and naturalists, about the growing campaign of the Chinese occupying forces, both military and civilian, to take back to China Tibet's heretofore untapped natural resources. Published reports told of the heavy felling of trees, frequently causing serious landslides and silting Tibet's major rivers, and the reckless slaughter of the formerly bountiful wild animals.

It became apparent that there was an urgent need to explore and further document the environmental changes we found in Tibet. Voluntary support groups were being organized in many countries to aid the Tibetan struggle for freedom. In many cases, these groups were formed by travelers who had visited Tibet.

In 1990, a conference focusing on environmental issues, called "Endangered Tibet," was held by Bay Area Friends of Tibet (BAFoT) in San Francisco. This conference presented information about the extent of environmental degradation occurring in Tibet as a result of the Chinese occupation. Of particular interest to many in attendance was the linking together of human rights violations and the environmental degradation—as it is an implicit right of all human beings to live in a safe, unspoiled, and healthy environment.[1] Conference speakers included Sinologist, Orville Schell, nature photographer, Galen Rowell; a climatologist, an ecologist, and a panel of Tibetans who had recently immigrated to the United States. The Tibetans related their personal observations of, and experience with, the devastation in their homeland. Following the conference, a small group of environmentally-minded participants came together in an effort to better understand what was happening on the Tibetan Plateau and to seek ways to help improve the situation.[2]

We were of the opinion that by producing an informative publication about the struggle in Tibet, we could educate and influence important decision makers in the United States Congress to become involved in improving the situation. The policies of the U.S. government toward China and the U.S. government's major role in the United Nations are crucial to the future of Tibet and the Tibetan people.

Initially, we believed that a publication showing images of Tibet before and after the occupation would deliver the most powerful message about the damage to the environment. In preparation for the book, one of the writers visited Dharamsala, India in 1992, the venue of the Tibetan Government-In-Exile and the residence of His Holiness the Dalai Lama. On quite short notice, His Holiness provided him with an interview, giving ample time for a discussion about our interest and goals.

Tenzin Atisha, Head of the Environment & Development Desk of the Department of Information and International Relations, was very responsive to our quest for more information regarding the current situation with the environment and use of the natural resources. We met knowledgeable government and non-government workers, and worked with translators for subsequent interviews.

Dharamsala has become a major axis in the world of Tibetan Buddhism. Its beginnings as a Tibetan center date back to the time of the original flight from Tibet, following the uprising in 1959 and the Chinese takeover of the country. Prime Minister Nehru generously gave this site to the Tibetans in exile. Many Tibetans have settled in this area, which is a reception center for refugees arriving from Tibet across the border into India, through Nepal or Bhutan.

Dharamsala is situated in an awe-inspiring setting in the foothills of the Dhauladhar Himalayas. It is both the seat of the Tibetan Parliament-in-Exile and the front of Tibetan Buddhist teachings and practice. The main religious and cultural institutions that had previously existed in Lhasa, and are now closed down, have been replicated here, but on a much smaller scale.

Everywhere in Dharamsala there are signs that this is a very special place dedicated to the preservation of Buddhist beliefs and Tibetan culture. Older Tibetans who fled during the invasion are seen twirling their prayer wheels and counting their rosary beads as they walk up and down the hilly roads leading to the main temple. Nearby is the residence of the Dalai Lama. The ever-present prayer flags flutter in the Himalayan breeze.

Time was spent meeting with Tibetan refugees. Those interviewed were from all classes; the group included monks, nomads, farmers, and former businessmen. While many had spent decades living in exile, others had recently trudged across the perilous high mountain passes seeking asylum and the freedom to practice their religion. Each wave of refugees had new and more foreboding information to relate about the occupation and the hardships it imposed. Spending time with these unfortunate but hardy people, and learning of their lives and personal experiences while in Tibet, served to shape the direction of this book.

We met with two young lamas who had fled Tibet during the latter part of 1990. They shared their personal histories of living as monks; one in the Drepung Monastery and the other in Sera Monastery in Lhasa, now under the domination of the Chinese "overlord." Formerly, the monasteries were more similar to universities than venues for retreat. However, now the daily routine requires the monks to spend their days at the most difficult and demeaning manual labor, leaving them no time to pursue their religious studies and devotional activities.

The monks described the continuing erosion of the Tibetan culture. The Chinese suppressed the use of the Tibetan language. The Han peoples (Chinese) and their culture had begun to dominate life to such a degree that it was feared the Tibetan culture would completely disappear.

The monks said they finally reached the point where they could no longer tolerate the persecution and oppression and joined with other monks in the major demonstrations held in Lhasa in 1987. They were imprisoned and beaten with sticks, kicked, and burned with cattle prods to the point of passing out. One escaped and the other bribed his way out by giving a Tibetan guard a picture of the Dalai Lama. Both then found a route over the Himalayas and escaped into Nepal and traveled on to Dharamsala, India.

We interviewed Rinchen, a stately Tibetan woman of gracious bearing. Her knowledge of the Tibetan community in exile was of incalculable help. She plays a leading role in this society, formerly holding the position of president of the Tibetan Women's Association (TWA), an organization of Tibetan women throughout the world dedicated to the preservation and well-being of Tibetans and their culture.

Rinchen told us about the recent arrival to Dharamsala of a group of ninety Tibetan Buddhist nuns from fourteen to forty years old. Over a two-year period they walked, enduring starvation and freezing weather, to Mt. Kailas in western Tibet, a mountain sacred to both Buddhists and Hindus. After circumambulating the mountain, they managed to escape over a dangerous pass into Nepal, finally arriving at Dharamsala.

When they arrived, they were almost at starvation point, frostbitten, and suffering from total exhaustion. After their recovery, they began their education and training so that they could play an important role in the refugee community. The serenity and high degree of esprit de corp of this group of refugees was remarkable.

We also went to the Tibetan Children's Village, where more than eight hundred children live. At the time of our visit, Tibetan parents were allowed by the Chinese to bring their children across the border for an education. Realizing there would be little chance for education in Tibet, especially one in which Buddhist beliefs and practices are taught, many Tibetans brought or sent their youngsters to the Children's Village. Because of the tense political situation, there is little guarantee that they will ever see them again.

The numerous children seen there were playing happily, many of them enthusiastically giving greetings in their beginning English. Their seeming resilience in this situation was remarkable in the face of the separation from their families. This trait of equanimity was observed among all the age groups seen in this outpost populated by refugees.

In our search for documentation material, we discovered that the Tibetan photographic archives had not been well preserved, and most of the images seen in Dharamsala archives dealt with Tibetan monastic life, religious art, and the lives of the more affluent city dwellers. And while Tibet is a literate society, Tibetan literature deals more with religious subjects, history, and legends instead of accounts of everyday life.

Although there were few photographs showing the recent damage to the environment, more documentation of the damage was becoming available. Even Chinese scientists were writing in professional journals about the negative ecological effects of the lumbering and mining industry, and the government policies behind it. Of a higher priority than the photos, however, was a need to document the native wisdom of the Tibetans; their skills in living in partnership with the land over the millennia.

In an era when the world is facing an international environmental crisis of serious dimensions, we believed it would be possible to learn some valuable lessons from Tibetans. Their experiences as successful nomads and farmers would perhaps teach us something important. Indigenous information about plants, conservation, and land management could be a benefit for mankind.

We realized that our observations concerning traditional rural life in Tibet would generate a more detailed understanding of the unique contribution of the Tibetan people. Therefore, we decided to make the lifestyles and experiences of Tibetan nomads, semi-nomads, and farmers the major focus of the book. These groups made up the vast majority of the Tibetan population before the occupation. Most of the information we wished to obtain was oral rather than written. So we needed to interview Tibetans who had lived as nomads, semi-nomads, and farmers before the occupation.[3] Our interviews took place in 1993, in a number of villages near Dharamsala in the state of Himachal Pradesh, India, a mountainous area where many Tibetans fled after 1959. Our research project was centered in Dharamsala.

Tsering Tsomo became our project director. An Indian-born Tibetan, Tsering was trained as a professional geographer in the United States. Her role was to locate and supervise a number of interviewers. They would interview exiles who had lived in rural areas of Tibet. A detailed questionnaire was developed and tested. The Tibetans would be asked about their environmental knowledge and lifestyles prior to fleeing their homeland. Our focus was on learning about the sources of the beliefs, knowledge, and survival skills that had sustained them. The team of Tibetan interviewers working under her supervision visited with men and women from most regions of Tibet. Our interviewers conducted and recorded the interviews in Tibetan, and then recorded translations in English.

In preparing for the interviews, Tsering and three members of the book project who were in Dharamsala met with a group of six nomads, semi-nomads, and farmers in an effort to identify any problems with our project design and improve the interview schedule (See photo, p. 112). During the meeting, which took all day, these engaging refugees shared a sense of heart-felt gratitude that foreigners had come from abroad to learn about their past and share mutual concerns about what has happened to their country.

Each, in turn, talked about their background and the circumstances of how they had fled to India. This was the first time they had an opportunity to be listened to concerning the present situation as refugees. While all six lacked even a basic education, they spoke with eloquence about how they missed their homeland and the satisfaction they derived from their former lifestyles and work. Each one expressed the wish that the world would learn about the plight of their people and help in the struggle to regain their country.

Dawa, a sixty-year-old farmer from the Chanthang, had recently arrived from Tibet and was able to describe how the methods of farming had been forcibly changed since the Chinese invasion. He had personally experienced much hardship because of the Chinese efforts to force Tibetans to accuse their neighbors of "counter-revolutionary activities." Dawa told us about his experiences:

> I was a farmer in Tibet, a *drokpa*, under the Chinese. I had nothing to eat, I had nothing to drink, and many other problems too. At present, because of His Holiness we all have enough to eat. Whether you are a rich person or a poor person, thanks to His Holiness's blessings, all of us have enough to eat—there is no one to be scared of. . . .
>
> You must surely tell the well-off, educated, and influential people in the world because no one bothers about anything unless it has something to do with themselves.... I have no influence and am now old. We have not been able to say things to anyone, and even if we did want to say something, there is no one who would listen to us. You have come here for everybody's happiness, and just as Buddha has said in his teachings, it is for the benefit of all sentient beings. . . it is really very useful for all Tibetans and we thank you sincerely. Now all of us hope to have freedom for our country, but there is no definite hope when we will get it.

NOTES

1. This is a value that has been forcefully presented by Mr. Galen Rowell, well-known nature photographer.
2. Two members of the group, representing Tibetan interests as part of the Non-Governmental Organizations, participated in the 1993 Rio Conference on the Environment providing documentation of the assault on Tibet's fragile environment.
3. Professor Melvyn Goldstein, an anthropologist at Case Western Reserve University, led a seminal study of the economic survival strategy of one group of Tibetan nomads. This study was useful to us, as it documented the ingenuity and the resilience of this group of nomads. However, we needed to obtain a broader range of first-hand information about nomadic and agrarian lifestyles with its joys and hardships. Melvyn C. Golstein and Cynthia Beall, *The Nomads of Western Tibet: The Survival of a Way of Life* (Berkeley, Calif.: University of California Press, 1990).

APPENDIX B

The Environment and Human Rights

Excerpts from a report on the study of Human Rights and the Environment, for the Sub-Commission on Prevention of Discrimination and Protection of Minorities.[1]

The United Nations Sub-Commission on Prevention of Discrimination and Protection of Minorities, of the Commission on Human Rights, [the Sub-Commission] is currently studying the nature of the interrelationship between human rights and environmental degradation, to determine whether and in what form human rights law should include an explicit environmental dimension.

The international community has acknowledged a number of substantive human rights that can be impacted by environmental abuse. It has also acknowledged procedural rights, the restriction of which can worsen environmental degradation by diminishing relevant communication between decision-makers, affected parties, and technical experts. These rights are accorded varying degrees of recognition and enforceability under international law.

In addition, both the International Covenant on Economic, Social and Cultural Rights, and the International Covenant on Civil and Political Rights confer upon all peoples the right to "freely pursue their economic, social and cultural development," and to "for their own ends, freely dispose of their natural wealth and resources without prejudice to any obligations arising out of international, economic-operation, based upon the principle of mutual benefit, and international law. In no case may a people be deprived of its own means of subsistence."[2] The most fundamental United

Nations document, the U.N. Charter, establishes as the purpose of the United Nations "to develop friendly relations among nations based on respect for the principles of equal rights and self-determination of peoples . . ."[3]

The Sub-Commission has determined that the Tibetans are a "people" distinct from the Chinese. In its resolution 1991/10 entitled "Situation in Tibet," the Sub-Commission referred to the "distinct cultural, religious and national identity of the Tibetan people," and called upon the Chinese government "to respect fully the Tibetans' fundamental human rights and freedoms."[4] The Chinese government also acknowledges this distinction by designating Tibetans as a "minority nationality" subject to different laws than the Han (i.e., the Chinese). For example, in its 1991 submission to the Commission on Human Rights, the Chinese government listed "various autonomous rights involving politics, economy, culture, and all other aspects of social development" guaranteed to the Tibet Autonomous Region, including "the right to independently protect, exploit, and use local natural resources according to law."[5] Thus, in applying human rights law to environmental matters in Tibet, Tibetans are entitled to the protections from the actions of the Chinese government accorded to any "people."...

The environmental impacts of the Chinese government's management of Tibet can be divided into two broad categories: those resulting from its removal of Tibet's natural resources for use elsewhere in China, and those resulting from the enormous resource demands created by the Chinese settlers who have participated in the government's policy of population transfer to Tibet.

Reports from Western observers who visited Tibet earlier in this century, before the Chinese occupation, emphasized the spiritual quality of the Tibetans' relationship to their land and their profound sense of the interdependence of life forms. Their Buddhism had one of its clearest expressions in the care with which they husbanded their natural resources. The Tibet that existed before Chinese occupation was a preindustrial, agrarian society. No one knows how Tibetans would have managed their transition into the modern world. What is clear is that the development and resource exploitation of the last forty years have reflected the Chinese government's values, in repeated violations of Tibetan practices and norms.

The unsustainable pace of deforestation, so far beyond the regenerative capacity of the land, is designed to meet the short-term resource needs of China's millions, leaving the Tibetans bereft of their timber and forest ecosystems, now and for foreseeable generations to come. The farming and grazing lands are being driven to support more settlers and more food exports than those fragile, high-altitude lands can sustain. Wildlife and native plants are being decimated because the markets for them remain uncontrolled, and because preservation of their habitats conflicts with the government's ambitions in areas capable of human settlement. . . .

Finally, requiring Tibetans to change their practices and manage their land in a non-sustainable way violates their cultural and religious integrity. A people's right to cultural integrity must include the right to act upon a cultural preference for biodiversity and healthy ecosystems in that people's land. Over time, violation of a peoples' spirit can have a coarsening effect; if the Chinese government continues to impose its values and practices, it is not inconceivable that Tibetans could lose their spiritual connection to their land. This would represent a cultural human rights loss as sad for Tibet's future as the loss of the land's biodiversity and ability to sustain its people.

NOTES

1. *Human Rights and the Environment: Preliminary Report Prepared by Mrs. Fatma Zohra Ksentini, Special Rapporteur, Pursuant to Sub-Commission Resolutions 1990/7 and 1990/27*, U.N. Sub-Commission on Prevention of Discrimination and Protection of Minorities, 43d Sess., Provisional Agenda Item 4, at 3, U.N. Doc. E/CN.4/Sub.2/1991/8 (1991).
2. International Covenant on Economic, Social and Cultural Rights, Part 1, art. 1, paras. 1 and 2, G.A. Res. 2200(A) (XXI), U.N. GAOR, 21st Sess., Supp. No. 16, U.N. Doc A/6316 (1966), 993 U.N.T.S 3 (Dec. 16, 1966), *entered into force* Jan 3, 1976; International Covenant on Civil and Political Rights, Part 1, art. 1, paras. 1 and 2, G.A. Res. 2200A (XXI), U.N. GAOR, 21st Sess., Supp. No. 16, U.N. Doc A/6316 (1966), 999 U.N.T.S. 717, *entered into force* Mar. 23, 1976 [hereafter International Covenants on Human Rights].

3. U.N. Charter art.1. As a United Nations member, the People's Republic of China is bound by the provisions of the Charter.
4. Sub-Commission on Prevention of Discrimination and protection of Minorities Res. 1991/10, Situation in Tibet, U.N. Doc. E/CN.4/1992/37, Aug. 23, 1991.
5. Reply of the Permanent Representative of China to the United Nations Office at Geneva, *Situation in Tibet: Note by the Secretary General submitted pursuant to Sub-Commission on Prevention of Discrimination and Protection of Minorities Resolution 1991/10*, U.N. Commission on Human Rights, U.N. Doc. E/CN.4/1992/37 at 15,16 (Jan. 5, 1992).

International Committee of Lawyers for Tibet (ICLT)

2288 Fulton St., Suite 312, Berkeley, CA 94704

Tel.: (510) 486-0588; Fax: (510) 548-3785; Email: iclt@igc.apc.org

APPENDIX C

Environment and Development Guidelines

[The Tibetan Government-In-Exile has created guidelines for international development projects in Tibet. The following are excerpts from the guidelines, which were published in 1994.]

Introduction

The Tibetan Government-In-Exile has, in the past, made its view known to foreign governments, international organizations, and others wanting to help develop Tibet. The concept is that, in principle, any assistance given to Tibetans in Tibet will be welcomed, provided it does not support the Chinese government's policies of population transfer and colonization of Tibet. This view comes from the belief that the Tibetan Government-In-Exile has a responsibility for the welfare of all Tibetans, both in and outside Tibet. . . .

In May 1992, the Chinese government announced the creation of a "special economic zone" in the so-called Tibet Autonomous Region. We believe that their objective is to stimulate foreign investment in the region to encourage settlement of Chinese in Tibet and to further consolidate Chinese political control in Tibet. It could also lead to further environmental degradation, depletion of Tibet's resources, and result in further human rights abuses.

His Holiness the Dalai Lama stated on March 10, 1993: "If the best interests of the Tibetan people are not kept in the forefront, there is a real danger that this policy will only promote and intensify the transfer of more Chinese into Tibet. This will further reduce the Tibetans to an insignificant minority in their own country, thus completing the thorough colonization of Tibet which will have serious consequences for its fragile environment."

Concerns with respect to the needs of the Tibetan people:... There should be meaningful Tibetan participation in all decision-making and implementation phases of the projects. Projects should take into consideration local conditions and needs as perceived by the local Tibetan people....

Development should refer not only to material and economic well-being for the Tibetans, but should also cover social, political, and cultural development. The Tibetan Government-In-Exile's concept of sustainable development takes into consideration not only the needs and requirements of the present Tibetan generation but also the needs of future generations....

The long-term goals of development policy and projects should be: (1) To transform the whole of Tibet into a zone of peace and nonviolence. This would be in keeping with Tibet's historical role as a peaceful, neutral nation, promoting stability and peace on the Asian continent; (2) To transform Tibet into a country based on democratic principles where every individual, irrespective of birth, sex, or religion, can freely practice his/her religion, culture, and economic activities; (3) To restore and preserve Tibet's fragile natural environment; and (4) To reverse the process of marginalization of Tibetans in Tibet and restore to Tibetans free control over their own destiny....

Guidelines for projects and investments: In light of the above objectives, the following guidelines are proposed for engagement in development projects in Tibet: (1) Development projects should be small-scale, decentralized initiatives over which Tibetans have control. Large-scale projects are discouraged. Promotion of appropriate technology enterprises is strongly urged; (2) All development initiatives should be preceded by social, cultural, and environmental impact assessments; (3) Projects that intensify and promote transfer of Chinese into Tibet should be opposed; (4) Development projects should use on a priority basis available trained and qualified Tibetans, and should provide effective and appropriate training and education to other Tibetans including, where appropriate, training in foreign languages; (5) Tibetan should be used as the working language of projects to the extent possible. It will be important for the development project staff to know the Tibetan language; (6) Projects should involve systematic and meaningful Tibetan participation in all phases including identification, design, implementation, monitoring, and evaluation; (7) Development projects must not directly or indirectly use prison or forced or child labor. They must not assist or help in experimenting, producing, and obtaining military or police equipment that can be used against the Tibetan people; (8) Special attention should be paid to education, welfare, and general upliftment of the position of Tibetan women; (9) The project managers, sponsors, and funding agents should regularly monitor and evaluate the projects to ensure that these guidelines and any conditions stipulated in the agreement are respected; (10) Projects should respect Tibetan culture and way of life as well as the aspirations of the Tibetan people; (11) Development projects should foster the self-sufficiency and self-reliance of Tibetans. Programs and projects should strive to draw on renewable resources available locally.

Priority Fields: Bearing in mind the above guidelines, the Tibetan Government-In-Exile recommends the following priority areas: (1) Rural health; (2) Rural education; (3) Strengthening and development of village-level development organizations and human resources; (4) Small-scale enterprises using appropriate technologies; (5) Small-scale hydroelectric projects providing power to Tibetan villages; (6) Training in traditional medicines; (7) Technical, professional opportunities abroad; (8) Adult literacy programs; (9) High-altitude research centers on nomadic farming, desert irrigation, livestock rearing, fodder, vegetation and solar energy, etc.; (10) Animal husbandry and dairy farming; (11) Horticulture; (12) Cultivation of medicinal plants; (13) Sustainable agriculture; (14) Traditional arts and crafts; (15) Ecologically sustainable tourism; (16) Woollen garment manufacture; (17) Forestry; (18) Cultural projects to restore monasteries, nunneries, libraries, and historical sites.

For more information and for discussion of specific proposals contact or consult:

Environment and Development Desk
Department of Information and International Relations
Central Tibetan Administration
Gangchen Kyishong
Dharamsala - 176215
INDIA
e-mail: diir@dsala.tibetnet.ernet.in
Tel: 0091-1892-22510
Fax: 0091-1892-24957

Tibet Support Organizations

International Campaign for Tibet (ICT)
1825 K Street, NW, Suite 520
Washington, DC 20006 USA
President: Lodi G. Gyari; Director: John Ackerly
Tel: (202) 785-1515 Fax: (202) 785-4343
E-mail: ict@peacenet.org
URL: http://www.savetibet.org

A nonprofit membership organization promoting human rights and democratic freedoms in Tibet. ICT monitors current developments in Tibet and reports the information to the U.S. Congress, human rights organizations, and the media.

Office of Tibet, New York
241 East 32nd St.
New York, NY 10016
Tel: (212) 213-5010 Fax: (212) 779-9245
E-mail: otny@igc.apc.org
URL: http://www.magicoftibet.com/tibetny

The Office of Tibet, in New York, is the oldest official agency abroad of His Holiness the Dalai Lama. This office handles the affairs of the Tibetan Government-In-Exile in North and South America. Established in 1964, one of the important functions of the office is to create a better understanding of the situation in Tibet and the aspirations of the Tibetan people. The office works to draw the attention of the international community to the plight of the Tibetan people in Tibet, and to establish contacts with governments and organizations. It is also responsible for those Tibetans residing in North America.

The Office of Tibet, London

Tibet House, 1 Cutworth St.
London NW83AF, U.K.
Tel: 0044-171-7225378 Fax: 0044-171-7220362
E-mail: tibetlondon@gn.apc.org
URL: http://www.tibet.com (The Official Website of the Tibetan Government-In-Exile)

The Office of Tibet, in London, is an official agency of His Holiness the Dalai Lama. Established in 1981, its main functions are to create a better understanding of the situation in Tibet and to draw the attention of world public opinion to the plight of the Tibetan people and the functioning of the exiled Tibetan government. The official website provides a wealth of information by the Tibetan government including updated lists of Tibet offices, support groups, and related organizations worldwide.

The Milarepa Fund

Tel: (888) MILAREPA
E-mail: info@milarepa.org
URL: http://www.milarepa.org

The primary focus of Milarepa's work is to educate people about the ongoing injustices in Tibet, and thereby awaken them to the forces causing these and other injustices throughout the world. Through various educational projects designed to integrate education, entertainment, and nonviolent activism, we hope to foster actions that will put an end to injustice through nonviolent means.

Students for a Free Tibet
241 East 32nd St.
New York, NY 10016
Tel: (212) 213-5011 Fax: (212) 779-9245
E-mail: ustcsft@igc.apc.org
URL: http://www.tibet.org.SFT
Contact: Diana Takata

Formed in August 1994 under the guidance of the U.S. Tibet Committee and the International Campaign for Tibet, Students for a Free Tibet is an international organization with chapters throughout the world. Through direct grassroots mobilization, SFT seeks to assist and give voice to Tibetans in their continuing struggle to overcome oppression. Students for a Free Tibet recognizes the Tibetan Government-In-Exile and its current leader, His Holiness The Dalai Lama, as the lawful government of Tibet. Students for a Free Tibet is dedicated to eliminating the suffering and oppression of all people through direct, nonviolent, and compassionate action.

Tibet House New York
241 East 32nd St.
New York, NY 10016
(212) 213-5592 Fax: (212) 213-6408
URL: http://www.tibethouse-ny.org
President: Robert A. F. Thurman

Tibet House New York is dedicated to preserving the living culture of Tibet. We feel that the wisdom and art of all nonindustrialized civilizations add meaning to life and enrich the emerging global culture. We share a special love for Tibet, its people, its spectacular highland, and its civilization of extraordinary beauty.

Tibet Online Resource Gathering
URL: http://www.tibet.org

The Tibet Online Resource Gathering is operated by the International Tibet Support Group community, providing information on the plight of Tibet and serving as a virtual community space for the movement.

Canada Tibet Committee
National Office
4675 Colbrook
Montreal, Quebec H3X 2K7 CANADA
Tel: (514) 487-0665 Fax: (514) 487-7825
E-mail: cantibet@tibet.ca
URL: http://www.tibet.ca
President: Thubten (Sam) Samdup

The Canada Tibet Committee (CTC) is a nonprofit organization that was formed in 1987 to work actively to end human rights abuse in Tibet and to bring the plight of Tibetans to the attention of people and governments. The CTC publishes a daily news digest: World Tibet Network (WTN) News on the internet. WTN rapidly disseminates information on Tibet activities and events throughout the world.

Geographic Map

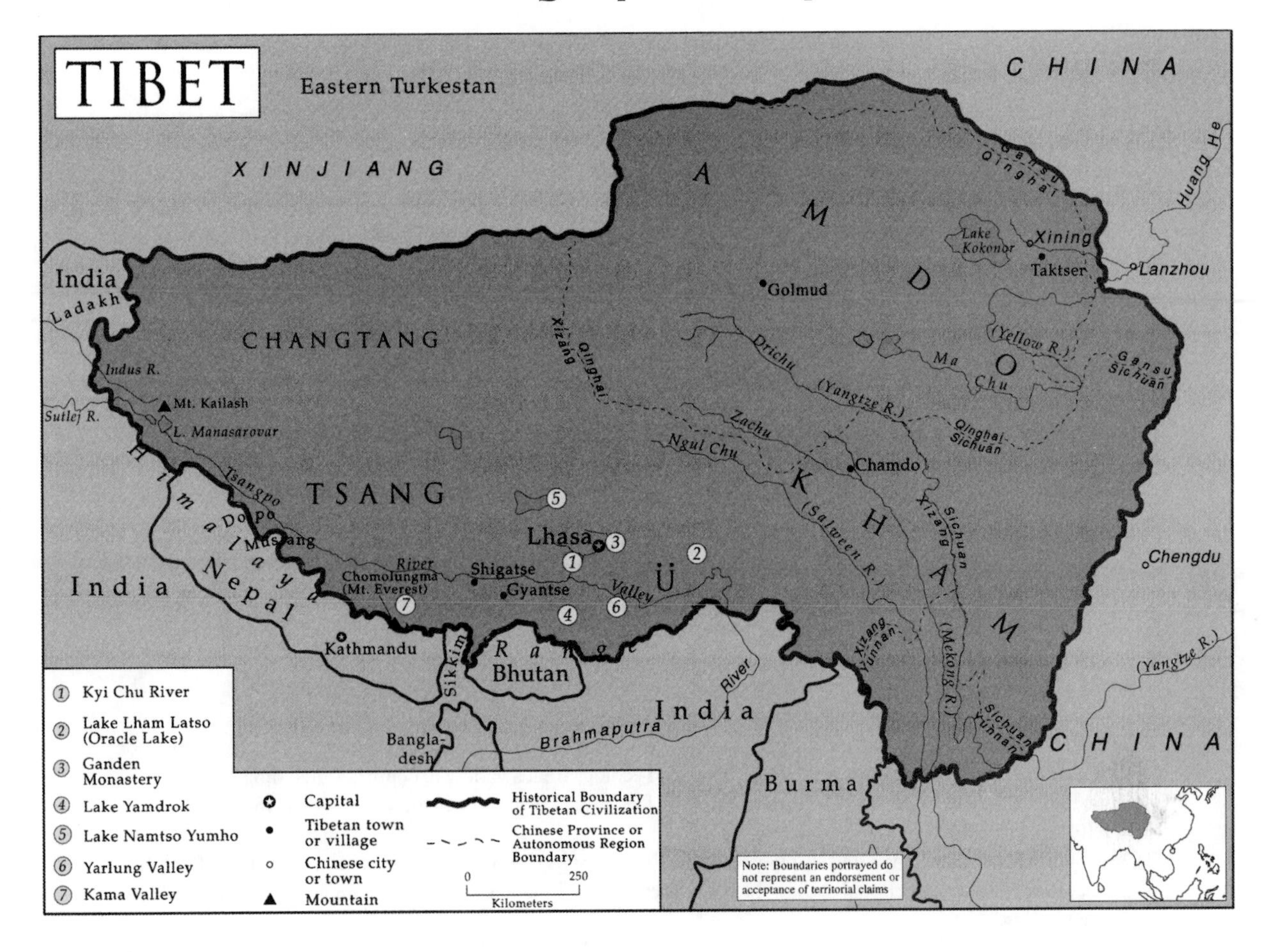

Bibliography

Journals

Canada Tibet Newsletter. Provides international news as well as information of interest to Tibet supporters in Canada.

News Tibet. A quarterly journal with political and cultural news about Tibet (free).

Snow Lion Newsletter. A quarterly publication with news, announcements, books, tapes, and Buddhist supplies (free).

The Tibet Journal. A quarterly publication of the Library of Tibetan Works and Archives (LTWA), devoted to the presentation of scholarly and general interest articles on Tibetan culture and civilization by Tibetans and non-Tibetans.

Tibet Monitor. A publication by the Tibetan Rights Campaign with articles and action items in support of the Tibetan cause.

Tibet Press Watch. A bi-monthly publication with up-to-date news about Tibet.

Tibetan Bulletin. The official bi-monthly publication of the Government-In-Exile of Tibet (free; donation to defray postage is appreciated).

Tibetan Review. A monthly publication about Tibet by Tibetans from New Delhi.

Books

Amnesty International. *People's Republic of China: Persistent Human Rights Violations in Tibet*. New York, N.Y.: Amnesty International, USA, 1995. A detailed account of China's human rights record in Tibet.

Ancient Tibet: Research Materials from the Yeshe de Project. "Tibetan History Series," vol. 1. Berkeley, Calif.: Dharma Publishing, 1986. This work contains useful background information on the geology, geography, culture, and history of Tibet.

Avedon, John F. *In Exile from the Land of Snows*. New York: Vintage Books, 1984. A moving account of China's brutal invasion of Tibet and the cultural genocide which followed.

Batchelor, Martine, and Kerry Brown. *Buddhism and Ecology*. New York: Cassell Publishers, Ltd., 1992. A useful resource exploring the relationship of Buddhism and ecology from a variety of countries including Tibet.

Capra, Fritjof. *The Web of Life*. New York: Anchor Books Doubleday, 1996. A fascinating new look at the patterns and relationships in the organization of living systems.

Carnahan, Sumner, and Lama Kunga Rimpoche. *In the Presence of My Enemies*. Santa Fe, N.M.: Clear Light Publishers, 1995. A Tibetan's personal account of the impact of the Chinese occupation, his imprisonment, and subsequent release.

Coleman, Graham, ed. *A Handbook of Tibetan Culture*. Boston: Shambhala, 1994. An indispensable guide to Tibetan centers and resources throughout the world. Includes histories of the main branches of Tibetan Buddhism and biographies of contemporary lamas and scholars, as well as academic, political, educational, cultural, and publishing resources.

Epstein, Israel. *Tibet Transformed*. Beijing: New World Press, 1983. For those interested in the Chinese view of Tibet following the invasion.

Goldstein, Melvyn C., and Cynthia M. Beall. *Nomads of Western Tibet: The Survival of a Way of Life*. Berkeley: University of California Press, 1990. A unique anthropological study of Tibetan nomads based on a field study of nomads from the Changthang region.

Gyatso, Tenzin, The Fourteenth Dalai Lama of Tibet. *Freedom in Exile: The Autobiography of the Dalai Lama*. New York: Harper Collins, 1990. An interesting and compassionate book about Tibet's fight for survival from the perspective of its political and spiritual leader, the Dalai Lama.

_____. *My Land and My People*. New York: Potala Corp., 1977. The Dalai Lama's personal account of his discovery as a reincarnation, his boyhood, training, life in Lhasa, and eventual flight with other Tibetans into India.

Gyatso, Tenzin, The 14th Dalai Lama, and Galen Rowell. *My Tibet*. Mountain Light Press, 1990. A stunning photographic essay of Tibet, supported by poignant observations and writings by the 14th Dalai Lama, Tenzin Gyatso.

Harrer, Heinrich. *Seven Years In Tibet*. Los Angeles: J. P. Tarcher, 1981. A unique and most fascinating account of life in Tibet before the Chinese invasion, as described by an Austrian mountaineer who lived in Lhasa for seven years in the 1940s.

International Committee of Lawyers for Tibet (ICLT). *Legal Materials on Tibet*. 2d ed., 1997. This report contains documents from: The United Nations; the governments of Tibet, China, and the United States; the European Parliament; as well as other nongovernmental bodies. Designed as a reference book for those investigating contemporary Tibetan issues, it is the most complete of its kind to date.

Johnson, Russell, and Kerry Moran. *The Sacred Mountain of Tibet: On Pilgrimage to Kailas*. Rochester, Vt.: Park Street Press, 1989. A beautifully photographed account of the pilgrimages and the significance of one of Tibet's sacred sites.

Kelly, Petra, Gert Bastian, and Pat Aello, eds. *The Anguish of Tibet*. Berkeley, Calif.: Parallax Press, 1991. An excellent, highly informative book discussing the current situation in Tibet covering human rights, environmental issues, and political and legal strategies, as well as Tibet's role in the world community.

Lazar, Edward, ed. *Tibetans-in-Exile Address the Key Tibetan Issue the World Avoids*. Berkeley, Calif., Parallax Press: 1994. Eight Tibetan exiles challenge the weakness of the international response to the occupation in Tibet. The choice, the contributors say, is clear. Either Tibet achieves national independence or the Tibetan culture and its people will become extinct.

Marshall, Steven D., and Susette Ternent Cooke, The Alliance for Reserach in Tibet (ART), *Tibet Outside the TAR: Control, Exploitation and Assimilation; Development with Chinese Characteristics*, 1997. Distributed as a CD-ROM available from International Campagn for Tibet (ICT), 1825 K Street NW, Suite 520, Washington D.C 20006. A very comprehensive survey (including over 2,700 pages if printed, photographs, maps, charts, tables) of the Tibetan areas which lie outside the Tibet Autonomous Region (TAR) and under four Chinese provinces.

Norberg-Hodge, Helena. *Ancient Futures*. San Francisco: Sierra Club Books, 1991. A well-documented examination of the impact of modern development on the Kingdom of Ladakh, known as "Little Tibet," in northern India.

Patt, David. *A Strange Liberation: Tibetan Lives in Chinese Hands*. Ithaca, N.Y.: Snowlion Publications, 1992. A very personal account of two Tibetans who survived to tell their stories of what it was like to be in Chinese hands during the worst years of the Chinese occupation.

Rowell, Galen. *Mountains of the Middle Kingdom*. San Francisco: Sierra Club Books, 1983. A well-written and photographed account of the mountainous region of central Asia as experienced by one of the world's premier photojournalists.

Sakya, Jamyang, and Julie Emery. *Princess in the Land of Snows*. Boston: Shambhala, 1990. An engaging personal story of one Tibetan woman's life and flight from Tibet which paints a multifaceted picture of Tibet's traditional culture, customs, and religious practices.

Schwartz, Ronald D. *Circle of Protest: Political Ritual In The Tibetan Uprising*. New York: Columbia University Press, 1994. The author examines detailed accounts of the Chinese occupation and its response by the Tibetan people.

Shakabpa, W. D. Tsepon. *Tibet: A Political History*. Dharamsala, India: Potala Publications, 1984. A Tibetan scholar's full account of the Tibetan nation from its earliest civilization up to the tragedy of the present Chinese occupation.

Stein, R. A. *Tibetan Civilization*. Palo Alto, Calif.: Stanford University Press, 1972. This book provides in-depth knowledge surrounding the Tibetan culture.

Taring, Rinchen Dolma. *Daughter of Tibet*. London: Wisdom Publications, 1987. An autobiography of a woman born in 1910 into the closely knit world of Tibetan nobility. The author covers the crucial fifty years up to 1959 in Tibet, including her escape to India and her work with refugees. She conveys the humor, resilience, and great faith so characteristic of Tibetan people.

Tibet, Environment and Development Issues, 1992. Dharamsala, India: Dept. of Information and International Relations, Central Tibetan Administration of His Holiness the XIV Dalai Lama, 1992. A comprehensive report on the environment of Tibet and land-use issues by Tibet's government-in exile.

Van Walt van Praag, Michael C. *The Status of Tibet: History, Rights, and Prospects in International Law*. Boulder, Colo.: Westview Press, 1987. A thorough and definitive discussion of Tibet's political history and legal right to self-determination.

Wei, Jing. *100 Questions About Tibet*. Beijing: Beijing Review Publications, 1989. The question and answer format makes clear the Chinese government's views on political and human rights issues.

PHOTOGRAPHERS CREDITS

Note: numbers refer to pages

Ackerly, John
67, 111

Bussell, Barbara
69, 72, 77, 104, 105,

Edwards, Andres
75, 112

Elchert, Carol
38, 43, 65, 73, 99, 109

Kling, Kevin
46, 68, 70, 100, 101,

McGee, Michael
33, 40, 42, 71, 79,

Office of Tibet
102

Rowe, Bradley
39, 44, 66, 74, 76, 78, 97, 98, 106, 107, 108,

Rowell, Galen
jacket, 34, 41, 47, 48, 103, 110

Sugden, Philip
80

Index

HEARTSFIRE BOOKS